CALF IN THE COTTAGE

Mr Matthews' face was weary. 'I'm fine,' he said. 'But I'm afraid the cow's having a few problems. Both of the calves are trying to be born at the same time and they're getting in each other's way. I'm going to need your parents' help, Mandy.'

Mandy ran across the farmyard to the house, her heart beating rapidly. She knew that twins were usually smaller than single calves, and being born early would mean that they were likely to be smaller still. Would they be strong enough to survive?

LUCY DANIELS

Calf
— *in the* —
Cottage

Illustrations by
Shelagh McNicholas

Hodder
Children's
Books

a division of Hodder Headline plc

Special thanks to Linda Kempton.
Thanks also to C. J. Hall, B.Vet.Med., M.R.C.V.S., for reviewing
the veterinary information contained in this book.

First published in Great Britain in 1996
by Hodder Children's Books
This edition published in 1997

10 9 8 7 6 5 4 3 2 1

A catalogue record for this book is available from the British Library

ISBN 0 340 71347 X

Typeset by Avon Dataset Ltd, Bidford-on-Avon B50 4JH

Printed and bound in Great Britain by
Clays Ltd, St Ives plc

Hodder and Stoughton
a division of Hodder Headline plc
338 Euston Road
London NW1 3BH

One

Mandy Hope tossed her blonde hair out of her eyes. There was a strong breeze blowing across the valley and cycling uphill was hard work.

'Come on, James. Let's take the short cut.'

'It's not a short cut. Not with all those hilly bits. That would just be hard work.'

'What do you call *this* then?' Mandy asked with a grin. 'Relaxation?'

James Hunter was Mandy's best friend. Both he and Mandy were mad about animals and spent a lot of their spare time looking after them. Mandy's parents were vets; they ran Animal Ark, the veterinary practice in Welford. They had adopted

Mandy as a baby after her own parents had been killed in a car crash, and Mandy thought they were the best parents anyone could wish for.

'Anyway, James,' Mandy continued, 'you're wrong. I tell you what though: if we take the short cut and you think I'm right, I'll let you look after my rabbits for a week.'

'Thanks, Mandy. And if *I'm* right?'

'I'll let you look after them for a fortnight.' Mandy grinned over her shoulder at James and pulled ahead of him. 'Come on, James! Race you to the Beacon!'

The Beacon was a Celtic cross, and a landmark for miles around. Their friend Lydia Fawcett kept goats in a smallholding nearby. Mandy smiled, as she remembered one particular goat, Houdini, who was probably even better at escaping than his namesake!

But today they were on their way to Barnall Mill, an old cotton-mill on the other side of the valley. The Barnall Mill trustees were running a pet show to raise funds for the mill, and one or two of Mandy's friends were entering their pets.

'Why didn't you enter Blackie for the pet show, James?' Mandy looked at her friend with a mischievous grin.

James grinned back but didn't say a word. Blackie was his adorable black Labrador; very beautiful but not very obedient. He'd probably cause chaos at a pet show!

They cycled on. Signs of spring were everywhere: trees in bud, daffodils in the hedgerows, and, best of all, lambs in the field.

'Look, James! Look at the lambs! Aren't they gorgeous?' Mandy and James stopped to watch them for a while, especially a little black one who thought he was cut out to be an explorer. They both laughed as he led his mother a merry dance round the field.

'Reminds me of you and Blackie,' said Mandy.

'I don't think Blackie's quite as well trained as that lamb,' said James, laughing.

They picked up their bikes and pushed on.

'Burnside Farm,' said Mandy, as they came to a wide five-bar gate. 'I haven't seen Mr Matthews for ages.'

Mr Matthews ran a small dairy farm, and Mandy loved the big farmhouse kitchen with its open fire and flagstone floor; but not as much as she loved the cows and calves that were Mr Matthews' pride and joy. And not as much as Mr Matthews loved them! Mandy's parents always said they had never

met a farmer who loved his animals as much as
Mr Matthews did.

'He's on his own at the moment,' said James. 'I
heard his son went off to Australia to sort out some
important family business. He was only supposed
to be gone for a month but he's having big
problems sorting things out. He's been gone for
ages now.'

'How come you know all about it?' Mandy asked.

'Walter Pickard was talking to my mum outside
the Fox and Goose the other day.'

'Poor Mr Matthews!' said Mandy. 'I wonder how
he's getting on with the farm, without his son.
Can we pop in and see?'

'Mandy,' James groaned. 'It's already twelve
o'clock and we're supposed to be having a picnic
before the pet show starts. We'll never get there
on time. And I'm starving!'

'But just think about Mr Matthews, all by
himself. And the animals! What about them?'

'Mandy,' James said patiently, as if Mandy were
six years old, 'Mr Matthews has been running that
farm since before our parents were born. He
knows what he's doing.'

'Still, I think we should go and see him. Just in
case.'

'You know what the matter with you is, don't you?' James didn't wait for a reply. 'You haven't got any animal problems to sort out. No puppies in the pantry, no kittens in the kitchen, no badger in the basement.'

'Look who's talking, James Hunter!'

'I am,' said James, grinning. 'All right, let's go and see Mr Matthews.'

They couldn't find Mr Matthews in the yard or outbuildings, so they wandered over to Burnside Farm. It was a lovely old house, built of grey Yorkshire stone. Tubs of daffodils stood either side of the big wooden door. James lifted the iron knocker and knocked loudly.

They heard the sound of Westie, Mr Matthews' West Highland terrier, as he came scrabbling and barking to the door. And Mandy saw Moggy, one of the farm cats, come running across the yard towards them.

'Hi, Moggy. Hi, beauty.' Moggy had long, fluffy, black fur and Mandy enjoyed the silky feel of it as she bent down to stroke the little cat. She put her hands behind Moggy's ears to give them a rub.

'James, her fur's all tangled and knotted. She's not been brushed for ages.' Mandy looked up at James, her eyes full of concern. She knew that Mr

Matthews adored his animals and made a good job of looking after them.

'Well, Westie sounds his usual healthy self,' said James.

Mandy frowned as she continued to work her hands over the cat's coat.

Mr Matthews was a long time coming, but at last they heard his voice.

'Quiet now, Westie. Quiet, boy.'

Moggy shot in through the door the minute it was opened – and Westie shot out! He barked up at Mandy and James and did a little dance at their feet. His short tail wagged furiously, and his little white body seemed to wag with it.

'Hello, Mr Matthews,' said Mandy. 'We were just cycling past on our way to Barnall Mill and we thought we'd pop in and see you.'

'Well, that's very kind of you. You'd better come along in.'

They followed Mr Matthews into the big farm kitchen. Westie was still doing a funny sort of dance, running backwards and forwards between his owner and the two friends.

Mandy looked round the kitchen. It looked as though nothing had been cleared away for a week! The sink was piled high with dirty pots and the table was covered with what looked like the remains of several meals. Absent-mindedly Mandy picked up a jamjar and screwed the lid back on.

Mr Matthews noticed her doing it. 'Aye, well. I've not been feeling up to much just lately. Just ignore the mess and sit yourselves down. I'll put the kettle on.'

'No, let me,' Mandy offered. 'You look as though you could do with a sit-down.'

'I'm not so old that I can't made a cup of tea for two honoured guests.' Mr Matthews smiled and Mandy saw the familiar twinkle in his eye.

Even so, she was concerned at how pale and tired the man looked, and at the mess in the kitchen. Whenever Mandy had come with her parents on routine checks of the animals, the kitchen had always looked spotless. Perhaps Mr Matthews just couldn't cope at the moment.

Mandy went to sit beside James on the old, comfy sofa in front of the fire. She saw that there were ashes in the hearth and the fire was almost out.

'Can I make up the fire for you, Mr Matthews?'

'No, thank you. I've to be out on the farm this afternoon. I was just having a lunch-time warm.'

Mandy sat back next to James. Westie sat on his

knee and gazed up at him adoringly. Mandy laughed.

'He's my number one fan,' said James, stroking the dog gently. 'Aren't you, Westie?'

Westie continued to gaze. His little tail flickered.

'He can smell Blackie, that's why,' Mandy replied. 'He thinks you're a strange-looking dog.'

Mr Matthews brought over two steaming mugs of tea. At the same time Moggy decided to jump on to Mandy's knee, just nudging the man's hand as he lowered the mug towards her. The mug seemed to do a backwards flip and in the next instant Mr Matthews' hand and arm were drenched in scalding tea.

'Are you all right?' Mandy and James said at the same time. They both jumped up. James bent to pick up the fallen mug and went to find something to clear up the mess. Westie ran round Mr Matthews' feet, clearly upset at all the commotion.

'No need to fuss! No need to fuss! I'm perfectly all right.'

But Mandy could see that he wasn't. Mr Matthews' arm was scarlet below the rolled-up sleeve and he was shaking from the shock.

'Let's get that arm under the tap,' Mandy said,

trying to take control of the situation calmly and quietly.

There was hardly room for Mr Matthews' arm with all the pots in the sink. James moved them away and, gradually, Mandy saw that the cold water was beginning to take effect. Mr Matthews seemed a bit less shaky.

James found a towel and passed it to Mandy.

'Thanks, James.' Mandy patted the arm dry. She was gentle as could be, but even so she saw Mr Matthews wince.

'I think we should call the doctor.'

'There's no need for any fuss.'

'It's not fuss, Mr Matthews. It's taking proper care.'

'I'm perfectly all right, Mandy. It's only a bit of hot water.'

They sat Mr Matthews down on the sofa and began to clear away. Mandy tidied and sorted, and James washed the pots. In no time at all the kitchen was looking clean and tidy. And James remembered that he was starving.

'Have you had anything to eat yet, Mr Matthews?' he asked.

'No. No, I'm not hungry.'

'You've got to eat something, Mr Matthews. I'll

go and get our picnic from the bike. You can share that.'

Mr Matthews sighed and closed his eyes. 'If you like,' he murmured, almost to himself.

Mandy followed James outside. 'Will you sort the picnic out while I have a look at the animals?' she whispered. 'I want to have a go at Moggy's coat, then check that the others have been fed.'

'OK, Casualty Officer Hope. But get a move on, I'm starving.'

'So am I!' called Mandy, already back in the kitchen.

'Have you got a brush for the cats, Mr Matthews? I thought I'd give them a going over while I'm here.'

'In the boiler room.' Mr Matthews pointed with his good arm. 'Through the door and first on your right.'

'And have you got any scissors?'

'Scissors?'

'Moggy's fur's a bit knotted. Some of it's quite bad. It won't brush out.' Mandy felt herself blush.

'Hanging on a nail in the boiler room.' His voice was very quiet, and Mandy saw that he looked a bit shamefaced. 'I've just not been feeling myself, you see. Couldn't get round to it somehow.'

Mandy wanted to put her arm round Mr Matthews and give him a hug. It wasn't his fault if things were getting too much for him.

Mandy found the brush and scissors easily enough. She also found Tabs, the old tabby cat, curled up on the boiler, fast asleep. She gave her a scratch under the chin and Tabs stretched herself luxuriously.

'It's a hard life, isn't it, Tabs?' she said with a smile. She ran her hands over the cat's coat. But Tabs was short haired and sleek and had managed to keep her own coat in good condition. 'I'll leave you in peace then, old girl,' said Mandy, giving Tabs a final pat.

The animals' bowls were on the floor of the boiler room, encrusted with stale food. There was a big enamel sink and she put the bowls in there to soak. She could wash them afterwards and feed the animals if necessary.

Back in the kitchen, James was spreading the picnic things out on the table. It was a good job they'd packed plenty. There'd be quite enough for Mr Matthews too!

But first Mandy wanted to sort Moggy's coat out. She lifted the sleeping cat on to her knee.

'Come on, Moggy. Let's make you beautiful

again,' she murmured gently.

The cat enjoyed Mandy's attentions. The knots were removed with one or two deft snips of the scissors. Moggy began to purr as Mandy brushed her coat, rhythmically and gently. In no time at all Moggy's coat was back to its former glory. Mandy was pleased with her efforts.

'She looks a treat,' said Mr Matthews quietly. 'A real treat. Thank you.'

James had organised lunch and Mr Matthews joined them although he didn't eat very much. Mandy noticed that his arm had begun to blister.

'I still think you should go and see the doctor, Mr Matthews.'

'Mandy,' Mr Matthews said firmly. 'I've got more new calves to look after than I know what to do with. I haven't got time to go to the doctor's.'

Mandy frowned. If he didn't go to the doctor's then his arm might get worse and he wouldn't be able to work. Then what would happen to the animals? She knew that they couldn't be neglected, even for a day.

'Have you got anyone who could help on the farm, Mr Matthews?' James asked.

'No, I'll manage by myself. Really, James, you're not to worry.'

'But what about the cows?' he persisted.

'The cows will be fine,' the old man said. 'And if you stop plaguing me I'll let you see the calves before you go.'

'Oh please, Mr Matthews,' said Mandy. 'Please could we see them?'

Westie, who'd been sitting under the table waiting for titbits, jumped up on Mandy's knee when he heard her excited voice. His tail wagged like a little flag.

'We're going to see the calves,' she told him, giving the dog a hug. 'And we'd better get cracking if we're to get to Barnall Mill on time.' Westie jumped from her lap as she stood up.

Together she and James tidied away the picnic things and washed the few plates they'd used. Then Mandy went back into the boiler room to wash the animals bowls.

'Shall we feed the animals before we go?' Mandy called.

'No, thank you.' Mr Matthews' voice was firm. 'They're not due yet and I can manage myself.'

Once outside, he led them across the yard to the wooden outbuildings. 'Come and look at this little beauty,' he said. 'Smashing little heifer, ten days old. Born at three o'clock in the morning so

I was up half the night with her.' Mr Matthews laughed. He didn't look as though he minded!

He pushed open the door to the calf box. 'I've called her Maisie,' he told the two friends. 'You've never seen such a beauty.'

She *was* a beauty; a little brown and white animal with a soft pink nose. She ran jerkily round the calf box when the three of them entered, but she soon stood still when she saw that they were standing quietly.

She came to sniff at Mandy's outstretched hand. Then her rough pink tongue came out and she tried to suck Mandy's fingers.

'It feels lovely,' said Mandy, laughing. 'Even though her tongue's so rough.'

'I think I'd like a calf for a pet,' said James, stroking the little animal's soft coat.

'I think you've got your hands quite full enough with Blackie and Eric,' said Mandy. Some time ago, she and James had found homes for a whole litter of unwanted kittens. Eric had been one of them, and he had grown into a much-loved cat. 'I don't think your parents would be too happy if you turned up with a calf,' she added. 'And I can't imagine a fully grown cow curled up in front of the sitting-room fire!'

Everyone laughed.

'Have you got any more cows due for calving?' Mandy asked. 'I love looking at them. They look like big round barrels.'

'We'd better not be too long,' warned James. 'Otherwise we'll miss half the pet show.'

'Won't take a tick,' said Mr Matthews. 'Come into the cubicle shed.'

Mandy and James followed Mr Matthews round the back of the calving boxes and past the milking parlour; then into the enormous cubicle shed. It was almost as big and high as an aeroplane hangar. The cows turned to stare at them lazily.

Mr Matthews ran his hand over a big brown and white cow. Then he turned to Mandy and James with a worried look on his face.

'She's started to calve already. She's having twins and she's not due for a good while yet.'

Mandy knew that even ten days could mean the difference between a healthy calf and one that didn't survive. And it was even worse when the cow was expecting twins.

Mandy's heart sank. It didn't sound too good at all.

Two

Mandy and James stood side by side, watching the farmer.

'Look,' he said. 'Look how her tail's raised. That's one of the ways you can tell they're about to calve.'

'Is there anything we can do to help, Mr Matthews?' Mandy asked.

'No, love. I think you'd best be off to that mill of yours. The day will be gone otherwise.'

'Are you sure?' asked James.

'Positive. I'm going to get Marble into one of the calving boxes so that I can keep an eye on her. She needs somewhere warm and safe to have her babies.'

Mandy knew that the calving boxes on Mr Matthews' farm were brick outbuildings about the size of large garages. The floors were covered with lots of fresh straw to keep the animals clean and dry.

'Can we come back later?' asked James. 'To see how she is?'

'You'll be most welcome if you've time. But go on now. Off with you.'

Mandy and James waved goodbye, then crossed the cubicle shed and went out into the yard.

The road to Barnall Mill was an easy downhill ride from Burnside Farm and it took the two friends only a few minutes to get there. When they arrived the place was teeming with people and animals. The spring sunshine was warm and Mandy felt her spirits rise.

'Hey, look who's over there!' shouted James.

Mandy turned to where James was pointing, and saw the sturdy, short-haired figure of their friend, Lydia Fawcett. She was wearing her usual corduroy trousers and jacket and was standing behind a stall, selling the wonderful goats' milk and cheese which she produced on her smallholding.

The two of them strolled over to see her.

'Hello, you two.' Lydia smiled at Mandy and

James. 'Have you just arrived?'

'Yes, we were held up at Burnside Farm,' said Mandy. She proceeded to tell Lydia all about Mr Matthews.

'Well, if there's anything I can do to help, just let me know. Perhaps he'd like some of my goats' cheese.'

'Thanks, Lydia,' said Mandy.

'You're not entering Houdini for the pet show are you?' said James with a grin, changing the subject.

'I don't think that would be a very good idea,' said Lydia, still smiling. 'And anyway, he's a working animal.'

'Working at escaping,' laughed Mandy.

'Oh, he's not so bad these days. Not since Ernie Bell built that strong new fence.'

'Mandy! Mandy Hope!'

Mandy turned to find Mrs Ponsonby bearing down on her. Mrs Ponsonby was a large woman who lived at grand Bleakfell Hall and wore pink spectacles. Her blue-rinsed hair was hidden under an enormous straw hat which sported clusters of cherries.

As always she was carrying Pandora, her Pekinese dog, and had Toby, her little mongrel, on a lead at her heels. Mrs Ponsonby was gasping and red in the face.

'Mandy, I'm so glad I've found you! You're the only one I can trust with my precious darlings!'

'What's the matter, Mrs Ponsonby?' asked Mandy.

'Well may you ask, my dear,' said Mrs Ponsonby, dramatically. 'Well may you ask!'

'What is it, Mrs Ponsonby?' James asked, trying hard not to grin.

'That unspeakable animal of Marjorie Spry's! Words fail me!'

'You mean Patch?' asked Mandy. Patch was a lovely little cat. It was Mandy and James who had persuaded elderly Marjorie and her twin sister, Joan, to give him a home in the first place.

James turned away, pretending to examine one of the stalls. His shoulders were shaking with laughter and he knew Mrs Ponsonby would have a fit if she saw him!

'Yes, I do mean Patch!' Mrs Ponsonby drew herself to her full height. 'You may know that I am president of the Barnall Mill Appeal Fund.'

Mandy didn't but she nodded anyway.

'Well, the wretched animal has eaten my speech!'

'Eaten your speech?' Mandy's voice was faint with suppressed laughter. She could imagine Mrs Ponsonby's words going round and round in poor Patch's stomach, like laundry in a washing-machine.

'Needless to say there's very little time to write another. Especially with two dogs to look after.'

'Can't you put Pandora down on the ground?' suggested James, who'd come back to join them now that he had his laughter under control.

'Certainly not!' said Mrs Ponsonby with a shudder of horror. 'You never know what she might pick up. Anyway, you must look after them for me, Mandy dear, whilst I dash off another speech. Think of it as your contribution to the Barnall Mill Appeal Fund.'

'Yes, of course, Mrs Ponsonby.' Mandy took Pandora and Toby from their anxious mistress. 'They're such lovely dogs.'

Mrs Ponsonby beamed. Any friend of her dogs' was a friend of hers.

'We'll just wander round if that's all right,' said James, taking Toby.

'Take good care of my little darlings.' She nodded her head graciously, as if dismissing them all, then sailed away like a galleon at full mast.

'I hope poor Patch hasn't got stomach-ache after eating Mrs Ponsonby's speech,' said Mandy.

'He's probably quaking with fear at the thought of having to face Mrs Ponsonby,' he replied.

Mandy and James wandered round, chatting to friends and looking at the animals. It seemed as though half of Welford was here, and all their pets! They met Kate, Mandy's friend from school, with her rabbits, and Tommy Pickard with his hamsters. Tommy was clutching a piece of paper with the number fourteen on it.

'I've lost Grandad and I can't find where I'm supposed to be,' he said. 'And the show starts in ten minutes.'

Grandad was Walter Pickard, a retired butcher who lived in the row of cottages behind the Fox and Goose. His wife, Mary, had died but he still shared his home with the three cats they'd both loved so much. He was a firm friend to Mandy and James, even though he could never remember their names.

'Don't worry, Tommy. He won't be far away,' said James. 'We'll help you find your place.'

They soon found the small pets section which was being judged in one of the marquees.

'Number fourteen!' yelled Tommy, spotting a space on one of the tables.

Mandy and James helped Tommy set up the hamsters' large cage; making sure the sawdust was smooth, positioning the water bottle exactly right. Tommy was very fussy!

'They're asleep,' he remarked gloomily, peering into the hamsters' bedding.

'Never mind,' said Mandy. 'Hamsters do sleep in the day; the judge will expect them to be asleep.'

'Will he?' said Tommy, brightening up a little.

'You bet,' said James, with a grin.

'Oh, there you are!' The voice boomed from the doorway of the marquee, and the three friends saw Tommy's grandad coming towards them.

'Hello, young miss, young sir. Hello, Tommy.'

Walter Pickard turned to the two friends. 'Tommy and I lost each other,' he explained.

'Yes, Tommy told us,' said Mandy.

'Well, thanks for looking after him,' said Mr Pickard.

Mandy and James waved as they went off to look at the other animals. There were white rats, gerbils, more hamsters, a chipmunk, even stick insects.

'I don't think I could cuddle one of those,' said

James, peering into the fish tank where they were kept.

'They're interesting, though,' said Mandy. 'Once you manage to spot them against the sticks.'

They strolled outside to the ring where the dog show was being held. But Pandora wouldn't stop barking at the other dogs.

'Come on,' said James. 'She's not going to be quiet till we move away.'

'Bet that Airedale wins,' said Mandy, following James reluctantly. 'He's a beauty.'

'Look, Mandy.' James gave her a nudge. 'There's one of the Spry twins with Patch.'

'Which one is it?' asked Mandy. 'Miss Joan or Miss Marjorie?' The two old ladies were hard to tell apart.

'I don't know. I can't tell the difference,' said James.

'Hello, Miss Spry,' said Mandy. 'I hear Patch has been eating Mrs Ponsonby's speech.'

Miss Spry went a little red and smiled sheepishly. 'I'm afraid Mrs Ponsonby left it on the table next to Patch's carrying basket. He must have pulled it through with his paw, bit by bit. He didn't really eat it though. Just chewed it up a little.'

'Well, that's a relief,' said James. 'I was just

waiting for Patch to miaow in Mrs Ponsonby's voice.'

They all laughed, and James turned red.

Mandy bent forward to have a look at Patch, completely forgetting that she'd got Pandora under her arm. She stood up quickly as soon as she felt the little dog wriggle and squirm at the sight and smell of the cat. But it was too late. With one final twist, Pandora jumped out of Mandy's arms.

'Oh, no! James! Help!'

James sprang after Pandora, who was running round in circles at the foot of the table. But he was hampered by Toby, who didn't see why he should miss out on all the fun. Toby tugged the lead out of James's hand just as James thought he had a hold on Pandora's collar. Now both dogs were tearing round like mad things.

Mandy dived after James, knocking the cat basket as she did so. It fell to the ground and they all heard Patch give an unearthly yowl. Before anyone could do anything they saw the door come unfastened. Patch escaped!

Toby tore after Patch, running right across Mandy's feet as he did so. This time Mandy was quicker. She dived once again and just managed to grab the end of Toby's lead, pulling him to a halt.

It was all rather undignified and Mandy lay sprawled flat out on the grass. She pulled herself up, brushed herself down and bent to pick up Toby.

'You're a bad boy, Toby,' she whispered in his ear. But Toby took no notice. He was too busy watching Patch and Pandora.

The two animals stood facing each other, Patch hissing and Pandora growling. Pandora stepped backwards, deep little growls in her throat. Patch stepped backwards too, his back arched and his ears back. Pandora stepped forwards, Patch stepped forwards; Pandora stepped back and Patch stepped back. It was as though they were practising some sort of dance. An amused crowd had gathered to watch the two animals.

Pandora flopped down on to her tummy and started to worm her way towards Patch, still with a little growl rumbling in her throat. The cat began to back away and hiss.

'This is brilliant,' said James. 'Do you think we should charge people to watch?'

'I think we ought to get hold of Pandora before Mrs Ponsonby gets back.'

'Oh, heck,' said James. 'I think you're too late.'

'Oh, my poor little Pandora! Oh, my poor darling!'

Mandy's heart sank as she saw Mrs Ponsonby pushing through the little crowd of people, the cherries on her hat bobbing wildly. She lunged to scoop the little dog up into her arms. But somehow, between clutching her hat and holding on to her handbag, Mrs Ponsonby missed. She did a little pirouette and collapsed, in a not very graceful heap, on to the grass.

'Oh, Mrs Ponsonby, I'm so sorry. Pandora just leaped out of my arms.' Mandy held out her hand but Mrs Ponsonby ignored it and struggled to her feet by herself.

'First my speech and now this! Just wait till I see your parents, Mandy Hope. I thought you were a sensible girl. I thought I could trust you!'

'But . . .' Mandy tried to defend herself but she couldn't get a word in.

She turned to see James handing Patch back to Miss Spry, then turn to pick up Pandora as calmly as if nothing had happened. Good old James!

'We're so sorry, Mrs Ponsonby,' Mandy heard him say. 'The dogs went wild when they saw the cat. There was nothing we could do about it.'

Mrs Ponsonby sniffed. But Mandy could see that she was a little soothed by James's good manners.

'I just hope they haven't picked up some dreadful disease,' Mrs Ponsonby said. 'Not everyone's as particular with their pets as I am. However, I have no wish to prolong this any further. I have my *speech* to think about.'

Mrs Ponsonby turned and swept away as if she were the queen.

'Oh, dear,' said Mandy. 'I didn't make a very good job of dog-sitting, did I?'

'Never mind,' said James. 'It wasn't your fault.'

'Hello again, young 'uns!' Mandy saw Walter Pickard waving at them from the door of the marquee. He was holding a large cat basket in one hand.

'Hello again, Walter!' she called, as he ambled towards them. 'I didn't realise you'd brought the cats. How are they?'

'Champion, thank you. But I've only brought Missy. Scraps and Tom are at home. I thought Missy might stand a chance in the cat show.'

'Yes, she's got a beautiful coat,' said Mandy.

Walter chuckled. 'Jolly well ought to have, the things she eats. Turns her nose up at everything except the best fish and chicken breast.'

'Oh, well, I hope she wins anyway,' said James, scratching Missy's nose through the wire of the basket.

'I enjoyed your little performance with those dogs of Mrs Ponsonby's. I thought it was one of the side-shows, put on specially.'

'Not exactly,' said James, going red. 'It was a bit of a disaster actually.'

'Oh, I shouldn't worry too much about that.' Walter chuckled again.

'I saw you cycling into Burnside Farm on my way down here,' he said. 'How is John Matthews?'

Mandy smiled. There weren't many secrets in a small place like Welford!

James told him what had happened that morning. Mr Pickard listened, nodding now and again. 'And of course it won't help with Sam Western pushing him to sell,' he said quietly.

'Sell the farm?' Mandy gasped. 'But Mr Matthews has always lived there.'

'You and I know that. But try telling it to Sam Western. You mark my words, he won't rest easy until he's either bought Burnside Farm, or made John Matthews' life a misery in the process of trying.'

Sam Western was a pretty ruthless farmer. He had no time for people or animals. The only thing he seemed to care about was how much money he could make.

Mandy and James stood silently. Things were worse than they'd thought.

'Anyway,' said Mr Pickard. 'I'm off now. See you again.'

The two friends spent the rest of the afternoon watching the judging. To their delight, Tommy Pickard's hamsters won first prize. Tommy could hardly stand still, he was so thrilled.

Mandy was also pleased to find that the Airedale had won the dog show. But when the winners of the cat show were announced, Walter Pickard looked a bit down in the dumps. Missy hadn't been placed.

'She's a finer cat than the winner, in my opinion,' he said.

Mandy and James tried to console him and he soon cheered up. They left him chatting to Tommy who still had a big grin on his face. At least one of the family had won a prize.

'Shall we get going now?' said Mandy. 'I think we've seen all we want to see, haven't we?'

'Probably,' said James. 'But we'll miss Mrs

Ponsonby's speech if we go now and I *really* don't want to do that.'

'James!' Mandy could hardly believe her ears. But when she looked at him she saw that he was laughing! She gave him a playful thump on the arm.

They walked over to the fence where they'd chained their bikes.

'Race you home,' said James.

But Mandy was thoughtful; not in the mood for racing.

'We've got time to go and see Mr Matthews again,' she said. 'I think we ought to pop in. It's on the way.'

'I wonder if the calves have been born yet,' said James.

'I hope so. I've never seen twin calves before,' said Mandy.

'Do you think they'll look like the Misses Spry?' asked James.

Mandy laughed. 'We could call them Marjorie and Joan.'

The two friends were pushing their bikes up the steep hill away from Barnall Mill. In the distance they could hear Mrs Ponsonby's voice booming through the microphone.

'Seriously though, James, I think we need to keep an eye on things up at Burnside Farm. Especially now that Mr Matthews has hurt his arm. It's not going to make it any easier for him. And I'm worried about the animals.'

'Well, that shouldn't be any problem,' said James. 'But I don't think you've got anything to worry about. Mr Matthews knows what he's doing.'

'Yes, but he doesn't normally have Mr Western to worry about,' said Mandy.

The two friends had reached the top of the hill. They mounted their bikes and rode on. It wasn't long before they saw the gate of Burnside Farm. They had just turned into it when a Land-rover approached them from the drive. It was going at breakneck speed and throwing up clouds of dust in its wake. As it came nearer they had to stand back against the fence to let it pass. It was Sam Western. His face was red and there was a look of pure rage on his face.

'I wonder what's bitten him?' asked James.

Mandy shrugged. She just hoped he hadn't upset Mr Matthews.

They left their bikes in the farmyard and began to look for Mr Matthews. Eventually they found him in one of the calving boxes with the calving cow. There was no sign of any calves.

'We've just seen Mr Western,' said James. 'He looked in a boiling rage. Are you OK?'

Mr Matthews' face was weary. 'I'm fine,' he said. 'But I'm afraid Marble's having a few problems. Both of the calves are trying to be born at the same time and they're getting in each other's way. I think this is going to be a long and difficult birth. I'm going to need your parents' help, Mandy.'

'Shall I go and phone for you?' asked Mandy.

'Aye. Thank you. I'd rather not leave this old lady at the moment.' He pulled gently at Marble's soft ears. 'Phone's on the kitchen dresser, Mandy.'

Mandy ran across the farmyard to the house, her heart beating rapidly. She knew that twins were usually smaller than single calves, and being born early would mean that they were likely to be smaller still. Would they be strong enough to survive?

Three

Mandy pushed open the door of the farmhouse and went straight across the kitchen to the dresser. At least she didn't have to look up the number of this vet!

It was Jean Knox, the receptionist, who answered.

'Jean, it's me, Mandy. Could I have a word with Mum or Dad, please? It's urgent.'

'I'm afraid they're both busy at the moment, Mandy. Is there anything I can do to help?'

Mandy's heart sank. But surely they couldn't be too busy to come and see a cow whose calves were in danger? She told Jean where she was and explained about the cow calving early.

'I'll try to get through to your dad, Mandy. He's out on a visit at the moment. Your mum's doing an operation and I don't think she'll be through for a while. And Simon is with her.'

Simon was the nurse at Animal Ark. He had not been out of college for very long but he was already an excellent nurse.

'Please get one of them as quickly as you can. I think this might be an emergency.'

'Will do, Mandy. Try not to worry.'

Mandy put the phone down quietly, a frown of concern on her face. She had expected her mum or dad to come quickly so that everything would be all right. They would know exactly what to do.

James was looking out over the calving box door when Mandy got into the yard. From inside she could hear Marble making lowing noises.

'What's happening?' she asked.

James shrugged his shoulders. 'The calves are trying to be born and Marble's trying to give birth. But Mr Matthews said something about them not being in the right position, and that's what's holding things up.'

'Poor things.'

'Anyway, did you get through to Animal Ark?' asked James.

'Yes, but it's going to be a while before anyone can get here. Mum and Dad are both busy. I'd better tell Mr Matthews.'

The farmer nodded grimly when Mandy told him the news. 'Ah well, that's the way it is with animals,' he said. 'You never know what's going to happen next.'

Marble gave another low of pain. She was getting restless and pacing backwards and forwards in the deep straw. Her eyes seemed to be half closed, as if she was concentrating.

'Poor old Marble,' Mandy whispered.

'You can feel one of the heads here,' Mr Matthews said, his hand pressing against Marble's flank. 'Do you want to feel?'

'Oh, yes, please!'

Mandy put her hand where the farmer indicated, and sure enough, she could feel a firm little bump.

'You're grinning like a Cheshire cat,' said James. But when he felt the little calf's head he was grinning too. 'It's amazing!' he said.

Mandy looked at her watch. It was getting late and they ought to be on their way home. But she didn't like to leave Mr Matthews all by himself. There must be plenty of jobs that needed doing round the farm. The only problem was that she didn't know how to do them!

She saw Mr Matthews look at his own watch.

'It's time I was getting ready for the milking,' he said. 'But I can't leave old Marble just now.'

'What will happen if you don't get the milking done?' asked James.

'Oh, I'll get it done all right,' Mr Matthews replied. 'But it might be a bit late and the cows don't like that; they get uncomfortable. I'd have got a relief milker in if I'd known this was going to happen.'

'What's a relief milker?' asked James.

'Someone who comes in and takes over for you. It can be a great help at times, but it's never the same. No one knows his own cows like the farmer. They're all different when you get to know them. They've got their own personalities, their own faces.'

Mandy smiled. When she thought of Mr Matthews' herd of brown and white cows it was hard to imagine being able to tell one from another. You had to work with them all day and every day, like Mr Matthews did, to know them individually.

Mandy looked at the farmer. He didn't seem at all tired now. He was probably too concerned about Marble. But he still had his sleeves rolled up and his arm didn't look too good. It was very red and blistered. Thinking about the accident it occurred to Mandy that Mr Matthews probably hadn't had a drink since lunch-time.

'Can I make you some tea, Mr Matthews? I bet it's ages since you've had any.'

'It is that, Mandy. I'd love a cup if you don't mind. And I'll try not to spill it all down me this time.' He gave a rueful smile.

'I'll have to be getting home,' said James. 'I promised Mum I'd walk Blackie before tea because he's not had a proper run today. Things were a bit hectic at home.'

Marble gave another deep low and Mr Matthews turned back to attend to her.

'I'll make Mr Matthews his cup of tea and then I'll go out on to the top road to see if I can see Dad coming,' said Mandy to James. 'I'll be able to get a lift back with him when he's finished here.'

Back in the kitchen, the previously sleeping animals seemed to have sprung to life. Moggy wound herself in and out of Mandy's legs and Westie came and sat by the sink and looked up at her, his little tail flicking every time she spoke to him.

'Are you two trying to tell me something?' she said. Westie gave a little yap and Moggy almost tripped Mandy up with rubbing round her legs.

'OK; I give in. Food coming up. But first let me put the kettle on, you rascals.'

She splashed water into the heavy old kettle and realised that there *was* something she could do. There were animals and humans who needed feeding.

In the boiler room she found Tabs still sleeping. But she woke as soon as she heard the rattling of food dishes. She jumped down on to the floor and began rubbing her head against Mandy's legs. Moggy had followed her into the boiler room and was competing with Tabs for Mandy's legs! Westie sat at the boiler room door looking alert and interested.

Mandy laughed. 'OK, OK, you lot. I'm going as fast as I can.'

There were cans of dog and cat food stored on a shelf and there was a tin-opener attached to the wall, so Mandy had no problem finding things. Soon, three contented animals were having their supper.

In the kitchen Mandy made the tea and looked for something to give to Mr Matthews. She found some ham in the fridge and made sandwiches. There didn't seem to be very much food in the house though.

Mr Matthews took the sandwiches and the mug of tea from Mandy's outstretched hands.

'You haven't got very much food in stock,' she said. 'I expect you're just about to do some shopping,' she added tactfully. 'But if you're not feeling up to it with your bad arm, the calves and everything, then maybe we can get some things when we go to the supermarket.'

Mr Matthews smiled. 'You're a very kind girl, Mandy Hope. I'll let you know if I need anything.' He sipped at his tea thoughtfully. 'We don't seem to be making much progress,' he said with a sigh. 'I hope it's not too long before the vet arrives. I've been trying to untangle the calves inside the mother but they're proper mixed up and I don't want to make it any worse.'

'I'll ride out to the road to see if I can see anyone coming,' Mandy said.

She bolted the calving box door behind her and set off to look for her mum or dad. It was quite a while since she'd phoned. Surely one of them would be here before too long? She didn't know how much longer Marble and her babies could wait!

Mandy cycled down the long driveway, somehow feeling more worried now that she was away from the farm. But as she turned out of the driveway and on to the main road she saw a Land-rover. She braked smartly and waved at the approaching vehicle.

She realised as it came nearer that it was Sam Western! She'd mistaken him for Dad! Mandy's heart sank as he slowed to a halt. He'd seen her wave and obviously thought she was waving at him.

An electric window glided downwards and Mr Western's head jutted out. He looked anything but friendly!

Mandy also saw Steve Barker, one of Mr Western's farm hands, sitting in the passenger seat. He was a young, dark-haired man, with a friendly, smiling manner. How could he bear to work for Mr Western and be shouted at all the time?

'I'm sorry, Mr Western. I thought you were my dad.'

'Well, I'm not!'

'I'm waiting for him to come and see one of Mr Matthews' cows. She's having a difficult time calving.'

Mr Western leaned as far forward out of the window as he could manage. Mandy took a step backwards.

'If Mr Matthews had been sensible and taken advantage of my very generous offer then he could be down in a nice little bungalow in Welford, instead of sweating out a living on that run-down farm of his.'

'But what about the animals?' Mandy asked. 'Those calves might die.'

'That's none of my business. And animals are just animals. He'll lose some money, that's all. Serve him right if you ask me. Incompetent old fool!'

Mandy stood with her mouth open as Mr Western drove away with a squeal of tyres. Her face was hot and she could feel tears pricking at her eyelids. Why was Sam Western always so horrible? How could anybody not care about two baby calves who might die before they were even born? And their mother might be at risk too. Mandy hadn't really thought about Marble before, but now she realised that it wasn't only the lives of the calves that were in danger. Poor old Marble might be in trouble too!

Mandy turned sadly and began to climb back on to her bike. There was no point in going any further along the road because she wasn't sure which way her dad would come. She cycled slowly back towards Burnside Farm and waited at the gate.

Before long she saw the Land-rover coming up the road out of Welford. This time there was no mistake. She recognised her father's dark hair and beard and waved both hands in the air. Mr Hope waved back and smiled. Mandy breathed a sigh of relief. Perhaps now everything would be all right.

Mr Hope drew the Land-rover to a halt and jumped out.

'Hello, love. What are you doing here?'

Mandy wheeled her bike round to the back so that her dad could lift it inside.

'Didn't Jean tell you that I'd made the call?' said Mandy, jumping into the passenger seat.

'Yes, she did. But that still doesn't explain what you're doing here.'

Mandy explained as briefly as she could the story of Barnall Mill, Mr Matthews and Marble.

They both jumped out at the same time, slamming the doors in unison. Dad went to fetch his wellies from the back.

In the calving box Mr Hope put on the green calving gown which he wore when he had calves to deliver. He knelt down beside Marble and began to examine her.

'These calves are in completely the wrong position to be born normally,' he said. 'They're still alive but I'm going to have to do an emergency operation to save them.'

Mandy listened carefully. Thank goodness he had arrived when he did. If he'd been any later the calves might have already been dead!

Four

'Mandy, can you phone Mum for me please?' Mr Hope asked. 'Tell her I'd like her to come up here as soon as possible to help with a caesarean operation.'

Mandy looked puzzled.

'Can't Mr Matthews help?'

'No, I sent him inside. I don't like the look of that arm of his. It will become infected if he doesn't get it seen to. Besides, I'd rather have another vet present.'

Mandy ran back across the yard to the cottage. Thankfully she got through to her mum straight away.

'I'll be right there, Mandy. Tell Dad I'll be with him in about ten minutes.'

Mr Matthews was sitting on the sofa, the plate of sandwiches in his lap. He was picking at them half-heartedly. He gave a big sigh and put the plate to one side. 'Seem to have lost my appetite,' he said. He looked pale and weary. Mandy wondered how much longer he could carry on.

'When does your son come back, Mr Matthews?' she asked.

'I don't really know. As soon as he's got things sorted out in Australia.'

Mandy smiled. 'I'd better go and tell Dad that Mum's on her way.'

'Tell him I'll be right over,' said Mr Matthews. 'Soon as I get my sea legs.'

Mr Matthews rose unsteadily to his feet.

Mandy put out a hand and he took hold of it gratefully. 'Don't you worry about me. It's those young calves and their mum we've got to worry about.'

Mr Hope was just coming out of the calving box as Mandy and Mr Matthews approached.

'Mum will be here in a few minutes,' she told him.

Mr Hope nodded. 'I need a bale of straw to put

the instruments on, John,' he told Mr Matthews.

'No, don't you go,' he said, as the farmer started to make his way round the side of the calving box. 'I can manage. That arm's going to get infected if you don't keep it clean and covered.' Mr Hope looked more closely at the old man's arm. 'And if you ask me, you're going to need some antibiotics. Who's your doctor?'

'Dr Mason, down in Welford.'

'Mandy, could you give Dr Mason a ring?' asked Mr Hope. 'Ask him if he'll come and have a look.'

Mr Matthews stood with his mouth open but he didn't say a word. He knew when he was beaten. Gentle Adam Hope could be very forceful when he chose!

Mandy got through to Dr Mason's receptionist straight away. She told Mandy that one of the doctors would be out to Burnside Farm as soon as possible. Mandy was relieved; it wasn't only Mr Matthews' animals that needed looking after!

Mandy heard her mother's four-wheel drive draw up as she closed the cottage door behind her.

'Hi, Mum! They're over here,' Mandy called.

Mrs Hope smiled. Her red hair was tied back and her face was freckled and pretty.

As soon as she entered the box Mrs Hope put down her bag and began to talk quietly to her husband.

'Poor old Marble. We'll soon have those babies delivered for you, old girl.' Mrs Hope talked quietly and gently to the animal.

Dad had covered the straw bale with a green cloth and was setting out his instruments. Mr Matthews had positioned a powerful electric light on the wall and it was focused on the corner of the box where Marble stood.

'Do you want me to help restrain her head?' asked Mr Matthews.

'No, thank you, John. We can manage,' Mrs Hope called. 'Mandy, why don't you go back in the kitchen? Or perhaps there's a job you could do for Mr Matthews.'

Mandy's heart sank. 'Can't I watch?' She'd seen normal deliveries of calves before, but she'd never seen a caesarean.

'Afraid not, Mandy. There's not much room in here and you're blocking the light standing by the door.'

'Come on, Mandy. How about feeding some calves for me?' Mr Matthews smiled, sensing her disappointment. 'And you can come and give a hand with the milking when you've finished.'

Mandy's heart lifted. Feeding the calves would help to take her mind off Marble.

'Now go and get yourself a piece of paper and a pencil out of the kitchen. Oh, and bring me a piece of chalk. You'll find it in the little blue jug next to the telephone.'

Mandy wasn't sure why she needed paper, pencil and chalk to help feed the calves, but she went to fetch them anyway.

'Over here!' Mr Matthews called when Mandy emerged from the cottage once more.

He was in a large shed which was attached to the stalls where some of the older calves were kept. Mandy stepped inside and sniffed deeply. There was a sharp, grainy sort of smell; a bit like a granary.

'It smells fantastic,' she said.

'That's the cattle cake and sugar-beet,' Mr Matthews said.

Cattle cake? Mandy looked down, half expecting to see slices of Battenberg or jam-and-cream sponge! But cattle cake was nothing like either of those. She bent down and scooped some of the little dark pellets into her hand. She sniffed them. They did smell good.

'Now, there's the cattle cake and sugar-beet pellets for the cows and older calves, then there are these smaller pellets for the younger calves. Write it down, lass. That's what the pencil and paper's for.'

So Mandy did.

'But how do I know which calves are which?' she asked.

Mr Matthews waved the piece of chalk in the air. 'This is where the chalk comes in,' he said. 'I shall chalk a number on each of the boxes and you can write the number down. Then you can make a note of what food to put in each of the numbered stalls.'

'Brilliant!' said Mandy. 'That's an excellent idea.'

She helped Mr Matthews to fill two buckets with the different kinds of pellets and then followed him into the first box so that he could show her what to do.

'I wonder what's happening with Marble,' Mandy mused.

Mr Matthews was quiet for a moment. 'She's in good hands, lass. Couldn't be better.'

Mandy knew how true that was. If she could be as good a vet as her mum or dad when she grew up, she'd be happy.

'Now then, you're to go in quietly to the boxes. The calves don't know you so you need to take care not to startle them. It takes time for them to get used to people. They get to know you after a while. Steady does it now.'

But when the calves saw Mr Matthews with food, they skittered towards him, knowing exactly what was coming! The two little brown and white calves followed him and his bucket. They were so eager that they tried to nose him out of the way before he'd finished emptying the pellets into the feeding trough.

'Just look at them,' Mandy laughed. 'Anyone would think they were half-starved!'

'They're like children,' Mr Matthews said. 'Children always feel half-starved, don't they?'

'They certainly do!' said Mandy. She realised that she hadn't had anything to eat since their picnic. And that was hours ago!

She stroked the head of one of the little calves. His coat was so soft and smooth. 'Their coats are really shiny, Mr Matthews. And so white.'

'Aye, well you know what they say? The brown should be brown and the white should be white. Meaning the brown bits should be very brown and the white bits very white. It's a sign of good health.'

'I'll remember that,' said Mandy.

'Anyway, I haven't got all day to stand chatting. You get on with that feeding now and I'll clean out the cubicle shed before milking.'

'Can't you leave it till the morning?' Mandy suggested. 'You're not very well and you ought to take it easy.'

Mr Matthews snorted. 'Since when has a working farmer been able to take it easy?' he asked. 'Do you know how much manure sixty cows produce in one day?'

'No.' Mandy had no idea.

'Between two and three tons every single day! Now tell me I should leave it till tomorrow!'

But how on earth was Mr Matthews going to get rid of three tons of manure? A dustpan and brush wouldn't do the job, that was for sure!

'I'm going to get the tractor, shift that manure.' Mr Matthews paused for a moment. 'What are you looking at me like that for,' he said. 'You didn't think I got it up with a dustpan and brush did you?'

Mandy burst out laughing. 'Oh, Mr Matthews. That's just what I was imagining!'

Mr Matthews laughed too. 'I'd be at it twenty-four hours a day at that rate. Thank goodness for tractors!' He turned to go but paused to bolt the calf-box door behind him. 'Cleaning, feeding and milking,' he said. 'That's what a dairy farmer's life is mainly about. Cleaning, feeding and milking. Just you remember that.'

'I will,' Mandy smiled. She picked up the buckets of pellets and went to the next calf box. Mr Matthews had chalked a number on the side: number two. Mandy consulted her list. These calves were quite young and not weaned yet. They'd need . . . ? Mandy looked at the buckets. She'd forgotten which of the pellets were which. Oh, heck! It was a complicated business being a dairy farmer.

'Mr Matthews!' She ran towards the cubicle shed where the farmer was walking towards his tractor, parked right at the far end. 'Mr Matthews. How do I tell the difference between the pellets?'

'Small ones are for the very young calves. Bigger ones for the older calves.'

'Thanks.' Mandy felt herself blushing. Fancy forgetting a simple thing like that!

Coming past the calving box where Marble was having her operation, Mandy was tempted to peer in. She badly wanted to know what was happening. She could see her parents but they were blocking her view of Marble. Mr Hope stood up and turned towards the door.

'One very small heifer and another about to be born. Off you go now.'

'Is it all right?'

'Off you go, Mandy,' Mr Hope repeated gently but firmly.

Mandy could hardly bear the suspense. But she knew Mr Hope was right. The welfare of the animals came before her own curiosity.

As she fed them, Mandy thought it was amazing how different all the calves were. The older ones tended to be more confident and came nuzzling at the food buckets. The younger ones were a bit more nervous and skittered round their boxes as she approached. She had to be careful not to make any sudden movements. She talked to them gently to gain their confidence. It was wonderful the way they responded. They were the most adorable little creatures!

She had another look at Maisie. The little calf was feeding from its mother, its tail wagging happily. There was no problem with Maisie!

It didn't take long to feed all the calves once she'd got the hang of consulting her list and making sure she was in the right box. It had probably taken Mr Matthews longer to explain everything to her than to do the job himself!

She looked at her watch. It was about an hour since her mum had arrived. Surely she could go and find out what was happening now?

Mandy ran across the yard, eager for news. She slowed down as she came to the door of the calving box. Marble was standing patiently as Adam Hope put some stitches into her shaved side. She'd been awake during the operation, but had been given a pain killer so that she didn't feel anything.

Emily Hope was bending over two little brown and white calves!

'Mum?' Mandy whispered. 'Is everything OK?'

Mrs Hope turned and smiled at the sound of her daughter's voice.

'We've got two little heifers, Mandy. But they're very small and Marble hasn't got any milk. They're going to have to be hand-fed with special fluids at first and it will be touch and go for a while. They're going to need a lot of looking after, especially the smaller one.'

'But they will be all right, won't they?' Mandy couldn't bear the thought that these little creatures might not survive. After all Marble had been through to have them, and after the fight they'd had to be born, it just didn't seem fair.

'We'll have to wait and see, Mandy. I can't make any promises. A lot will depend on these first few days. Normally they'd get the very best start with Mr Matthews as nurse, but Dad tells me he's not well.'

Mandy explained about the scalded arm.

'And he didn't really look very well when we first arrived this morning,' she said. 'Everywhere was a mess and he seemed tired.'

Mrs Hope looked thoughtful. 'He's not as young as he was, Mandy. It must be very hard work for him just now, with his son being away. But he's tough. He'll be all right.'

Mandy smiled. Her mum knew just how to make a person feel better.

'Shall I go and tell Mr Matthews about Marble?'

'I think you'd better. They're his animals.'

Mandy made straight for the cubicle shed, eager to tell Mr Matthews about the lovely new calves. She couldn't hear the sound of a tractor – *maybe he's started milking*, she thought.

The cubicle shed was clean, but she couldn't see any sign of Mr Matthews on his tractor. She noticed that the big double doors at the end of the shed were open, so she headed that way. As she came through them, out into the open air, she saw the tractor only a few metres away, its engine ticking over quietly. Mr Matthews was probably about to drive the tractor back to its parking place in the shed.

'Mr Matthews! Mr Matthews!' Mandy called. But there was no reply. Wondering what was happening, Mandy wandered up to the side of the tractor. There she found Mr Matthews slumped across the tractor seat, his eyes closed.

Five

Mandy ran as fast as she could out of the cubicle shed and across the farmyard.

'Mum! Dad!' she called. 'It's Mr Matthews. He's fainted or something. Come quickly.'

'All right, Mandy. I'm on my way.' Emily Hope followed her daughter quickly across the yard.

Mandy breathed a sigh of relief when she arrived back at the tractor. Mr Matthews had his eyes open and he was trying to sit up.

'I went a bit dizzy,' he said. 'Must have fainted.'

Mrs Hope put out an arm and helped the farmer down from the tractor. At the same time, Mandy looked up to see the tall figure of Dr Mason húrrying across the shed.

'Good timing,' said Emily Hope, smiling at the doctor.

Mr Matthews was standing now and brushing down his jacket.

'I'm perfectly all right now, thank you very much. No need to fuss. Just a little bit of a turn.'

'Let's get you inside, John,' said Dr Mason.

'I haven't time for that,' Mr Matthews protested. 'I've got a herd of cows overdue for milking. They can't be kept waiting any longer. And what about Marble, Mrs Hope? How's she doing? Have you got those calves delivered yet?'

'One thing at a time, John. Let's get you into the house then we can sort out what needs to be done.' Dr Mason and Mr Matthews went inside, leaving Mandy and Mrs Hope staring after them.

'He's going to have to get a relief milker,' said Mrs Hope quietly. 'He'll never manage otherwise. And those calves are going to need a lot of nursing if they're to survive.'

'I can do that, Mum,' Mandy offered.

'No you can't, Mandy. Not by yourself. You can't be here during the night for one thing.'

'Why not?' Mandy had visions of her and James in sleeping-bags on the kitchen floor. It would be great fun! They could do the night feeds.

'Because I wouldn't allow it,' Mrs Hope answered firmly. Mandy knew it would be pointless to argue. 'Now, do you want to see those calves or not?' asked her mum.

Mandy followed her mother back into the calf box where her dad was feeding one of the calves by hand. He had inserted a tube into the calf's stomach and was putting fluid into the tube with a syringe.

'What's happening, Dad?'

'I'm giving her a special feed. Her stomach's too young to tolerate milk just yet so she'll need to be fed with this special scour formula for a time.'

'It's not as good as the mother's milk, of course, but it's pretty good stuff,' Emily Hope added.

Mr Hope had covered the two little calves with straw to keep them warm.

'Are they going to be all right?' Mandy asked.

'Well, they're very quiet now because they've had quite a rough time being born,' her mum answered. 'They need time to recover. The little one's very weak and we're a bit concerned about her. But they look like a couple of fighters to me.' Mrs Hope smiled her lovely warm smile, her green eyes lighting up.

'Your hair's all fiery in the light,' Mandy noticed.

Mrs Hope laughed. 'I'll feel a bit more fiery when I've had something to eat,' she said. 'There's a casserole waiting for us in the oven.'

Mandy's stomach did a flip. Food!

Mr Hope had inserted a tube into the other calf's stomach now. He moved some of the straw away and put his head against her side.

'Why are you doing that?' Mandy asked.

'I'm listening for stomach noises,' he said. 'To check that I've not inserted the tube into the lungs by mistake.'

Marble was standing at the side of her two calves, nosing them gently. The stitches from her operation stood out against the bare, pink skin where her coat had been shaved.

'Is Marble all right?' Mandy asked.

'She's fine,' her mum said. 'She's going to be absolutely fine.'

'Why don't you two get off home,' Mr Hope said. 'I can manage by myself now.'

'Good idea,' said Mrs Hope. 'That casserole beckons.'

'Well, don't you two eat it all before I get back,' Adam Hope said with a grin.

'You'd better not be too long then,' Mrs Hope warned.

Dr Mason was leaving just as Mandy and Mrs Hope stepped outside.

'He's got a bit of an infection but he'll be fine once the antibiotics get working,' Dr Mason told them. 'He just needs to keep that arm clean and rest up a bit. Neither of which are very easy for a dairy farmer! At any rate I've persuaded him to get a relief milker in for tonight and tomorrow.'

'Well, that's good,' said Mrs Hope. 'We'll pop in and see him before we leave.'

Mr Matthews was putting the phone down as they entered the kitchen. His arm had a dressing on and there was a smile of relief on his face.

'Managed to get Ted Wilkins to take over the milking for a while. He'll be right over.'

'Oh, well done, John.'

'How's Marble?'

'She's doing fine. You've got two heifers,' Mrs Hope told him.

'How are they shaping up?' he asked anxiously.

'Well, it's early days yet,' Mrs Hope replied. 'But we're a bit concerned about the smaller one. She's rather weak.'

'Dad's just feeding them now, Mr Matthews,' Mandy told him. 'They're gorgeous! James thinks we ought to call them Marjorie and Joan after the Spry twins.'

Mr Matthews threw back his head and gave a roar of laughter. 'That's the best idea I've heard in a long time,' he said. 'And I think it's about time I went and had a look at them. I've spent far too long messing about with this arm.'

'We'll be off then, John. One of us will pop in and look at Marble and the calves tomorrow. Goodbye.'

Mrs Hope closed the door quietly behind them.

'He's got his hands full,' she murmured, almost to herself.

Mandy didn't say anything. But she was determined to do everything she could to help Mr Matthews and his animals.

Six

The next morning Animal Ark seemed to be bursting at the seams!

'I think folk must have waited for the Easter holidays to get all the routine stuff done,' said Jean Knox, the receptionist. 'They all seem to be coming in for injections and so on.'

Mandy smiled. Animal Ark always seemed to be busy, but she rather liked this extra hubbub of animals and people. It made the place seem so alive.

Mandy wanted to get to Burnside Farm as soon as possible but she had her chores to do first. She was just off to start helping Simon to clear out the bedding in the residential unit when she almost tripped over Emily Hope who was coming out of the surgery. She was talking to a woman with shining blonde hair. Both of them were looking very serious indeed.

'What a gorgeous dog!' Mandy exclaimed, bending down to stroke the woman's Great Dane. She didn't have to bend very far. He was enormous!

'Yes, he is gorgeous,' his owner agreed. And Mandy saw that her eyes were filled with tears. Poor thing. What on earth could be wrong with the animal?

Mrs Hope ushered the woman through the waiting-room and out of the main door, talking quietly to her all the time.

'What's the problem?' Mandy asked.

'Bruno is a beautiful dog but very old. His owners are going abroad to live. It'd be expensive to take him and he hates travelling anyway. They're trying to decide whether they should take him with them and put him through the trauma of the journey or whether they have him put down. He's so old he might not live that much longer anyway. Very difficult decision. And I can't make it for her.'

Mandy sighed. Poor dog . . . poor owner!

'Oh, Mandy!' Jean Knox was beckoning from behind the counter at reception. She held up a big brown parcel. 'I nearly forgot. Would you pop this into your gran's for me? It's for the Women's Institute jumble sale. Thought you wouldn't mind, as you're always popping in and out.'

Mandy smiled but her heart sank a little. It would be nearly lunch-time before she got to Burnside Farm at this rate. And she had to pick up James on the way.

'I've just made some flapjack,' Gran said as she and James arrived at the door of Lilac Cottage. 'You must have smelled it.'

Mandy could certainly smell it now! A delicious aroma wafted through the open doorway and even though she and James had brought a picnic lunch, the offer of fresh flapjack and coffee was too good to resist.

They sat comfortably at Gran's kitchen table with the sunshine streaming in through the window. Grandad had joined them at the table and they all sat in comfortable silence.

'Mornings like this make you glad to be alive,' Gran remarked, a contented smile on her face.

Glad to be alive. Gran's remark reminded her of the two little calves up at Burnside Farm. And of Mr Matthews. Mandy began to tell Gran and Grandad the whole story. James interjected every now and then with a detail or two.

'He's a good lad, John Matthews,' Grandad remarked. 'And it sounds to me as if he could do with a bit of help.'

'He certainly could!' Mandy agreed.

'Well, I've just been shopping and I got in some extra supplies for the caravan. But we're not planning to go away just yet so I don't see why John shouldn't have them.'

'Oh, Mrs Hope, that's really kind of you,' James said.

Gran patted him on the cheek. 'Get away with you,' she said. 'What are neighbours for?'

Mandy grinned. Nobody could wish for better neighbours than her gran and grandad.

'Mind you, I don't suppose Sam Western's making life any easier for him,' said Grandad.

Mandy frowned. Somehow the very mention of Sam Western's name made her anxious.

'Mr Western wants to buy Burnside Farm. And from what I understand he's putting a lot of pressure on Mr Matthews to sell,' said Grandad.

'Yes, we heard.' James paused with his coffee-cup halfway to his mouth. 'But why would he want Burnside Farm? He's got enough land of his own.'

'Some people never have enough,' Gran muttered. 'Some people are plain greedy.'

'Well, the fact of the matter is,' said Grandad, leaning back in his chair, 'Highfield Farm's for sale. It's going to be auctioned and Sam Western wants to buy it. But to have as much land as he'd really like he needs to buy Burnside Farm as well. It's right next door to his own land, and to Highfield Farm; it would make him one of the biggest landowners for miles around.'

'And never mind who gets hurt in the process,' Gran said angrily.

'Well, surely it's up to Mr Matthews' son, too,' Mandy said.

'Ah, well now,' said Grandad, in a mysterious voice, 'that's the other half of the story. Apparently Mr Matthews' aunt in Australia has left him a tidy sum of money, but it's all wrapped up in a legal wrangle. That's what his son is doing there; if young Alan can sort it out then Mr Matthews stands to gain quite a lot of money.'

'Well, I hope Alan Matthews does manage to sort things out,' said James. 'And I hope he comes back very soon with a lot of money.'

'Aye,' said Grandad. 'Alan Matthews wants to buy Highfield Farm too. But if they don't get the money in time then it's Sam Western who'll win the day. And then he'll probably find a way of driving the Matthewses off the land.'

'But money won't make any difference to those two little calves. They won't get a better carer than Mr Matthews whether he's rich or poor,' said Mandy.

'That's true,' James agreed. 'And we ought to be getting up there if we're going to be any help.'

'I'll just get those groceries put in a box,' said Gran, standing up from the table. 'And Mandy, tell Mr Matthews I'll be over to see him tomorrow. So if there's anything he wants he can give me a ring and let me know.'

'Oh, I nearly forgot,' Mandy cried. 'I've got a parcel for you from Jean Knox. It's for the jumble sale.'

'Good old Jean,' said Gran. 'She never forgets.'

Mandy handed the parcel to Gran, who then went to pack the groceries for Mr Matthews. There were tins and packets, some fruit and cheese, butter and a great big loaf of freshly baked bread.

'That should keep him going for a day or two.'

Gran stood back with a look of satisfaction on her face.

'Thanks, Mrs Hope,' said James. 'He'll really appreciate it.'

Mandy gave her a kiss on the cheek. 'You're a lovely gran, Gran,' she said.

Gran smiled. 'Don't forget to tell Mr Matthews that I'll be over tomorrow.'

'I won't,' said Mandy.

James was outside, strapping the box to the back of his bike.

'There, that should do it.' He stood back, admiring his handiwork.

'Come on, James. Let's go.'

James wheeled his bike down the path after Mandy, stopping to wave to Mandy's grandparents who were standing by the gate.

It was a glorious cycle ride up to Burnside Farm. The sun was warm and everywhere was bright and gleaming.

'Your gran was right,' said James. 'It does make you feel glad to be alive.'

Mandy felt her excitement growing as they came to the gate of Burnside Farm.

'I wonder how Marble's doing,' she called to James.

'Just what I was thinking,' he replied.

When they got into the farmyard, James and Mandy parked their bikes and made immediately for the calf box. There was Marble and there were her two babies, still lying down and covered with straw. Mr Matthews was kneeiing beside them, tube-feeding one of them as Mr Hope had done.

'You've just missed your dad, Mandy. He left about ten minutes ago.'

Mandy knelt down beside Mr Matthews and stroked the smaller calf's head. 'What did he say?' she asked anxiously.

'This little one's still a bit dodgy.'

Mandy didn't think that Mr Matthews looked too good either. He looked tired and weary.

'And how are you?' James asked. He was moving to the back of the box, towards Marble.

'Now, just be careful, young James. You should never get between a mother and her calves.'

'Sorry,' James said. He moved carefully to the back of Marble, away from her babies. He began to pull gently at her ears. 'Anyway, how are you, Mr Matthews?'

'Oh, fair to middling. You know.'

Mandy and James smiled.

'Would you like to have a go?' Mr Matthews asked.

'Oh, yes please!' said Mandy.

'Careful does it then.' Mr Matthews refilled the syringe from the container of liquid and passed it to Mandy.

'Put it into the end of the tube. That's right. Now just make sure you don't shove it in too quickly; otherwise you'll make the poor little lass sick.'

Mandy gently squeezed the end of the syringe to inject into the tube. The liquid would travel down the tube and into the calf's stomach.

'How long will you have to do this for?' James asked.

'Two or three days, I should think. Until they're on their feet and ready to feed from a bottle or their mother.'

'Can I have a go?' James asked.

Mandy refilled the syringe and inserted it back into the tube. 'Here you are,' she said, handing it over to James.

'Thanks.' James kneeled down, his face growing serious at the prospect of feeding the calf. As always, his spectacles were halfway down his nose.

'Marble looks OK,' said Mandy. 'And the wound looks nice and clean.'

'She's doing very well,' said Mr Matthews. 'She's making a good recovery.'

Mandy went and stood beside Marble, heeding the farmer's instruction not to stand between mother and babies. The cow looked at Mandy with her big brown eyes. Mandy stroked her gently.

'There, that's that done,' said Mr Matthews. 'Two well-fed calves.'

'If you give us ten minutes, Mr Matthews,' said Mandy, 'there'll be three well-fed humans. I made a picnic for us. Shall I go and put the kettle on?'

'That sounds like a very good idea to me,' said Mr Matthews.

'Me too,' said James.

'Well that's really kind of your grandmother,' said Mr Matthews, unpacking the box of food that Gran had sent. 'I'll give her a ring after lunch and tell her so.'

'She's coming to see you tomorrow,' said Mandy. 'You could tell her then.'

Mr Matthews sat down in one of the big old armchairs by the fire. 'I'll ring her after lunch even so. I like to be prompt with my thanks.'

'It won't take two of us to get lunch ready. Can I do something on the farm while James gets on with it?'

James, who had already made a pot of tea and

set the table, scowled at Mandy with mock ferocity.

'It's just about ready. I got on with it while you were talking your head off.'

'OK. OK.' Mandy put her hands up in a gesture of surrender. 'Don't shoot.'

James grinned and threw the tea-towel at her. Mandy caught it and folded it back into the box.

'I'll tell you what you can do, Mandy,' Mr Matthews said. 'Do you see that big book up on the shelf? Could you pass it down for me. There are a few photographs you might be interested in.'

Mandy handed down the heavy old book and Mr Matthews took it carefully.

'We'll have a look at these over lunch,' he said.

Mandy had packed an enormous picnic. There were cheese and pickle sandwiches, packets of crisps, thick, moist slices of Gran's flapjack, and a selection of fruit. Not to mention cartons of orange and apple juice and a big pot of tea. James had set it all out carefully on the big blue-and-white checked tablecloth.

Westie sat at the foot of the table, staring up expectantly. Where there was food, there was Westie!

'Are you hungry, old boy?' James bent down and

stroked the little dog. At the sound of his name, Westie sat up on his haunches in a begging position.

Mandy and James laughed.

'Well, this is a spread fit for a king,' said Mr Matthews, heaving himself out of the armchair. He looked at the meal with pleasure. 'I've not had a table set like this since Alan went to Australia. Very tastefully done, James. Are you going in for catering when you leave school?'

'No,' James muttered, going a little red at the praise. 'Computers or animals. I can't decide which.'

'Animals,' said Mandy, as they all sat down round the table. 'No contest with computers. You can't cuddle a keyboard. And you can't have the satisfaction of caring for it and watching it get well again.'

'I could do with a granddaughter like you,' said Mr Matthews. 'You'd be marvellous round the farm. And young James here.'

'We can both be your stand-in grandchildren for a while,' said Mandy. 'We'd like to help out as much as we can till Alan comes back. We've got all of the Easter holidays.'

'If we could just learn what to do,' put in James,

eagerly. 'Then we could let you take things easy for a while – till your arm gets better.'

Mr Matthews smiled. 'You're a couple of eager young beavers aren't you?' Mr Matthews smiled. 'Be prepared though. I'll treat you like apprentice farm hands and teach you properly.'

'Great,' said Mandy. 'That's just what we want.'

Mr Matthews tapped at the old photograph album. 'This farm's been in my family for generations. It would break my heart to see it go.'

'But it's not going to go!' said Mandy. 'We won't let it. Will we, James?'

'We certainly won't,' said James, pushing his glasses up his nose earnestly. 'We'll do everything we can. And get more help if necessary.'

'Rally the troops,' said Mandy, waving her sandwich in the air.

'Hang on a minute, you two. You make it sound like the siege of Burnside Farm.'

'The siege of Burnside Farm, by Mr Matthews' friends! That sounds like a good sort of siege to me,' said Mandy.

'Aren't you going to eat anything, Mr Matthews?' asked James, changing the subject. 'You've hardly touched that sandwich.'

'You have to eat to keep your strength up,' put in Mandy.

'The arm's feeling a bit better now but I'm still not very hungry. Thirsty but not hungry. Dr Mason told me to drink plenty of fluids. You wouldn't mind pouring me another cup of tea, would you, James?'

Mr Matthews opened the photograph album and Mandy gasped as she saw the old brown and white photographs.

'These are my grandparents,' he said, pointing to a photograph of a man and woman standing by an enormous bull with a rosette pinned to its halter. The woman was wearing a long skirt and an old-fashioned bonnet and the man stood with one foot on an old stone water trough, holding a pipe in his hand.

'That bull won best of breed at the very first Welford Show. Won it the following two years as well.'

'You weren't born then, were you, Mr Matthews?' asked James.

'I'm not *that* old!' he said, laughing. 'This photograph was taken over a hundred years ago. The men in our family live a long time, but not that long!'

Westie got quite excited at the sound of laughter. He turned round two or three times at the foot of Mr Matthews' chair and then with one jump, leaped on to his knee.

'Down, Westie! Down, boy!' Mr Matthews commanded.

But Westie wasn't going without a little something to see him on his way. Before Mr Matthews could stop him, Westie had stolen the sandwich off his plate and jumped back on to the floor. He dashed off into the far corner of the kitchen and gulped the sandwich down.

'Westie, you're a bad boy,' scolded Mr Matthews. 'Bad boy, Westie!'

The little terrier lay his ears flat against the side of his head and backed into the corner as far as he could go.

'Oh, just look at him,' said Mandy. 'He knows you're cross with him.'

'Aye, but he still thinks he can get away with murder.' But the farmer's features softened and he couldn't help smiling at the terrier. Westie's ears lifted and he trotted back to the table.

'You're a monster, Westie,' said James, leaning down to pat him. Westie leaned against James's legs and gazed up into his face.

'You said he was your number one fan,' said Mandy, with a grin.

Mr Matthews was leafing through the photograph album. He showed Mandy and James photographs of the family and farm that spanned over a century and up to the present day.

'So you see,' he said, closing the album with a sigh, 'this farm's not just a job to me, it's a way of life. It's where I belong.'

'You just wait till Alan comes back,' said James. 'Everything will be all right then.'

'There are some people who don't want it to be all right,' said the farmer, mysteriously. 'There are some people who are pleased with the way things are going at the moment because they'd like to see this farm fail.'

Mandy knew he was talking about Sam Western.

'But things will be better when Alan gets back, won't they?' asked Mandy.

'If he can sort out some legal matters then everything will be fine and dandy. Our problems will be solved. Now then, are you apprentices ready to start work?'

'You bet!' they both shouted.

Mandy and James cleared up the kitchen while Mr Matthews went out to look at the calves. It wasn't long before they joined him.

But when they went inside the calf box they could see immediately that something was wrong.

Seven

Mr Matthews looked up at them; he wore a worried expression.

'I think I'm going to have to phone for your parents, Mandy,' he said. 'I don't like the look of this little one at all. She's taken a turn for the worse.'

Mandy and James both knelt down beside the little calves. Mandy gently moved the straw round the smaller one's body, covering it with more straw to help it keep warm. The animal didn't respond to her touch and its ears were cold when she felt them. Mandy knew the ears were a good guide to a calf's temperature.

'Look,' said Mr Matthews. 'Marble's completely ignoring her. Animals know when their babies aren't going to survive.' His voice was sad.

Mandy's hand ran gently across the calf's head, brushing and stroking its smooth coat. 'Don't die, little calf,' she whispered. 'Please don't die.'

Her eyes blurred with tears. She didn't want Mr Matthews to see. He was a working farmer; what would he think if he saw her crying? She turned her head away.

The little calf was still breathing but her eyes were closed and she was very still. Mandy knew the calf was in serious danger.

'It's all right, Mandy.' She felt Mr Matthews' hand on her shoulder, patting it roughly. Somehow it made the tears fall faster.

'There's been many a time when I've cried over an animal.' Mr Matthews' voice was comforting. 'There's no point in doing the job if you don't feel for them. Don't be ashamed of it.'

Mandy pulled a clutch of tissues from her pocket. She wiped her eyes and blew her nose.

She heard Mr Matthews stand up and unbolt the door. 'I'm going to phone Animal Ark,' he said.

It was quiet in the calf box. There was only the

sound of Marble moving in the straw.

'Look,' whispered James.

'What?' Mandy looked round. The other calf had lifted her head and was looking round, alert and lively.

'Oh,' Mandy breathed. 'Just look at her.'

She glanced at James's smiling face and saw that he was red-eyed too. It was good to know that he felt the same as she did.

Mandy reached her hand out to stroke the lively little calf. 'I think you're going to be on your feet soon,' she said. The little calf seemed to nod in agreement.

'What's that noise?' said James suddenly.

Mandy listened. She couldn't hear anything.

'It's dogs barking. Listen!'

Yes, now she could hear. But these weren't friendly barks. These barks sounded loud and wild. She could hear Westie's frantic response from the other side of the cottage door.

She and James rushed out of the calf box, bolting the door behind them, and ran across the yard. Sam Western was just coming into the farmyard, his two stocky white dogs tearing ahead of him, growling and barking.

They heard Westie whining frantically, his claws

scratching at the cottage door. From the cubicle shed the cows were making an unsettled lowing.

The two dogs tore across the farmyard towards the shed.

'No! Stop them!' Mandy shouted. She had awful visions of the dogs running loose among the cows, biting, snapping, injuring them. 'No!' she called again.

James was ahead of her as she reached the cubicle shed. She realised, with a sigh of relief, that it was protected by a barred metal gate. The dogs could not get in, although they scrambled frantically at the gate as they tried.

Mandy's fear turned to anger. What was Sam Western doing, letting his dogs loose in another farmer's yard? He knew perfectly well what damage they could have caused.

'What the heck's going on?'

Mandy turned at the sound of Mr Matthews' furious voice.

'What d'you think you're doing, Sam Western? Get those dogs on a lead.'

Mandy and James stood, open-mouthed, as the two farmers confronted each other. Mr Matthews held his head high, anger written across his face. Mr Western was smiling, as if this was a pleasant social occasion.

'You heard me. Get those dogs on a lead.' Mr Matthews' voice was quiet now. Quiet and very, very angry.

'If you insist, John. This is a right of way, I believe. Across your land and through the farmyard?'

Mr Matthews nodded grimly.

'Well then, I was just exercising my right to use it. No problem, is there?'

'You have every right to walk across my land,' said Mr Matthews. 'What you don't have is the right to bring your dogs to worry my cattle.'

'What an absurd accusation, John. I shall put my dogs on their leads, of course. But I shall be walking through your yard as often as I please. It's a very pleasant walk. And my dogs seem to like it too.'

Mandy's heart sank. What was Mr Western up to now? Was he trying to make Mr Matthews so miserable that he'd sell the farm just for a bit of peace and quiet?

Mandy and James watched Mr Western slip his dogs on to their leads and stride away.

'That's Sam Western's idea of discussing things,' muttered Mr Matthews. 'If he can't get his own way by fair means then he'll choose foul.'

'But surely there's no discussion,' said James. 'You don't want to sell and that's that. End of story.'

'You tell that to Sam Western, my lad. It would be the end of the story to most people. But not to him.' Mr Matthews turned and started to walk towards the calf box.

'I didn't know there was a footpath through your farm,' said Mandy.

'Oh, yes.' Mr Matthews stopped for a moment. 'It's an ancient right of way. And I've no objection most of the time. It's just occasions like this when I wish it wasn't.'

Mandy and James followed Mr Matthews over to the calf box. All three of them looked over the top of the door. The weak calf looked no better. She lay completely still in her bed of straw.

'I've called her Bella,' said Mr Matthews. 'I thought she ought to have a name. And as it looks as though she may not make it, I figured it wasn't such a good idea to name her after one of the Sprys.' He shook his head. 'It's not looking good at all.'

Mandy's heart sank still further. Although she knew Mr Matthews was speaking the truth, she didn't want to hear him say it.

'Your dad'll be over before too long. But before he comes I'd better show you what to be getting on with. The first thing is fresh bedding for the calves. They should have had it earlier but I've not had the time or energy.'

Mr Matthews looked drained, Mandy noticed. His face was white and he held his scalded arm slightly to one side, as if it bothered him.

'Are you all right, Mr Matthews?' she asked. 'How's the arm?'

'Oh, not too bad. A bit painful still but that'll pass. Dr Mason's popping over again this evening. I don't know, a sick calf, an ailing farmer and a neighbour who's doing his best to make life difficult.' Mr Matthews sighed.

'I shouldn't worry about Mr Western,' said James. 'He's being a pain at the moment but he knows he can't make you sell if you don't want to.'

Mr Matthews nodded. 'Come on, you two. This isn't getting the calves seen to, is it? Let's look sharpish.'

Mandy and James had to haul fresh bales of straw from the barn. They found that there were separate blocks of straw in each bale, and they had to pull these apart and spread them over the floors of the calf boxes, on top of the old straw.

'It's dead springy,' said James, jumping up and down. 'I could almost sleep on it myself.'

'Bad luck,' said Mr Matthews. 'We've got too much work to do!'

The three calves in the box looked on in astonishment at James's performance. One of them ran into the corner of the box, as if deciding it needed to keep a safe distance.

'That's one very sensible calf,' laughed Mandy.

'There's another,' said James, pointing.

Mandy saw one of the other calves at a little trough built into the wall. It had a small lever which the calf had to press with its nose to get the water.

'That's clever,' said Mandy. 'I wonder how they learn to do it?'

'Calves are curious animals,' said James. 'They like being nosy and investigating everything. I expect they nudge and nose at it until they get the water by accident. Then they think: Hey presto! Water! I'm a genius!'

Mandy laughed. 'You sound quite the expert,' she said.

James pushed at his glasses. 'I've just been doing a bit of reading,' he said.

Their next job was to feed the calves. As Mandy had already done this she was able to show James what to do. She still had the list that she'd made and she and James were able to get on quickly.

They went to look for Mr Matthews to see what needed doing next. He was in the yard next to the cubicle shed in the middle of what seemed like hundreds of cows!

Some of the cows were suspicious of Mandy and James. They looked warily at the new farm hands out of big brown eyes; some of them backed away when either of them came near.

'Just don't make any sudden movements that could frighten them,' said Mr Matthews. 'They'll soon get used to you, but you're strangers at the moment. Give them time.'

Mandy thought the cows were wonderful creatures. She loved their faces with the beautiful eyes and enormously long eyelashes. And yes; she could see that they didn't all look the same, not when she looked at them carefully.

Mr Matthews called them over. He was unfastening a wire at one end of a big pile of silage.

'It smells like vinegar,' said Mandy, wrinkling her nose.

'Well, it is pickled grass,' said Mr Matthews. 'Although it hasn't got vinegar in it, of course! Now, we have to move the wire back so the cows can get at it,' he said. 'It's an electric wire and it stops the cows eating more than you want them to. You push the wire back as far as you want them to eat and then let them get on with it.'

Mandy and James watched as Mr Matthews pushed the wire back against the wall of silage.

'There. That should do it,' he said.

They left the cows in the little yard. The ones at the front of the queue were now happily munching away at their silage. The others milled around, waiting patiently for their turn.

'First come, first served,' James told the cows.

'You'll just have to get out of your cubicles more quickly next time.'

Mandy laughed. One cow was looking at James as if she understood every word he said.

Their next job was the cubicle shed. All the cubicles had to be swept out and have fresh sawdust put down. A few of the cows were in the stalls and Mr Matthews had to move them out so that the cubicles could be swept.

'I generally sweep them out in the morning,' Mr Matthews explained. 'But my arm was playing me up a bit so I left it till now. The brushes are propped against the wall, if you want to go and fetch them.'

The cubicles were concrete platforms, raised above the level of the main floor. Once the cows had climbed into them there was no room for them to turn around, so when they wanted to come out they had to step backwards. Mandy and James were fascinated to see how delicately they edged their back hooves to the back of the platform and felt their way down on to the floor.

'They almost look as though they're going to stumble and fall,' said Mandy.

But they didn't. They were more sure-footed than they looked.

'They don't exactly hurry, do they?' said James, with a laugh.

Mandy and James set to, cleaning out the cubicles. But it was no small task. There were sixty cows on the farm and that meant sixty cubicles! By the time they were about halfway through, Mandy's arms were aching.

'Do you think we could stop for a cup of tea, James?' she called. James had started at the other end of the cubicle shed and was working quite a distance away from Mandy.

'That sounds like a very good idea to me.'

But this was a different voice. And it was right behind her!

'Dad! You made me jump!' said Mandy.

'That's because you're so busy wielding the yard brush,' said Adam Hope, with a smile. 'Anyway, I need to take a good look at this calf.' Mr Hope left her to get on with her work.

Mandy put down her brush. She needed to find out what was happening to the sick calf. 'Come on, James,' she called. 'Let's go and see what's happening. We can finish this later.'

'OK.' James walked up to her, red in the face with exertion. 'I'm dying for a drink,' he said.

'We'll get one after we've seen the calf,' said Mandy.

James rolled his eyes; with Mandy it was always animals first.

When they reached the calf box they saw the two men kneeling down in the straw with their backs to them, so that they couldn't see what was happening. They both knew better than to call out with questions or to go into the calf box at that moment.

'Mandy, why don't you and James put the kettle on,' Dad called, without turning round. 'I think we could all do with a cup of tea.'

'OK,' Mandy said, in a small voice. She had that sinking feeling in her stomach again. She suddenly felt sure that Bella was not going to survive.

'Come on, Mandy,' said James quietly.

'If there was only something we could do,' said Mandy, after she'd put the kettle on. 'I feel so useless.'

'You can't win through every time,' said James. 'You know what your mum and dad say: learning to accept that you can't do anything for an animal is one of the hardest lessons of all.'

Mandy sighed. She knew James was right. But it was never easy. It was never going to be easy.

After they'd made the tea, they sat quietly in the big armchairs in front of the fire. Westie was curled up quietly at James's feet and Moggy had jumped on to Mandy's knee and gone to sleep. It was as though the animals knew how they felt. Mandy said as much to James.

'Animals do know how you're feeling,' he said. 'I'm convinced of it.'

But Mandy didn't need any convincing. She agreed with James wholeheartedly.

'I'll go and see if they want to have their tea in the calf box,' she said to James. It was no good. She just couldn't wait any longer for news.

But at that moment the door opened and the two men walked into the kitchen. Westie jumped up and went running over to Mr Matthews, wagging his tail.

Mr Matthews bent down to stroke him, his face grim. Mandy didn't have to ask. She knew from the two men's faces that the little calf was lost.

'I'm afraid she'd dead, Mandy,' she heard her father say. 'She was just too small and weak to survive. She put up a good fight but she didn't make it.'

Mandy felt the tears come again. She could hear the two men talking quietly, and the chink of their cups against the saucers. James was very quiet.

'Can I go and see her?' she at last managed to say.

'No,' said Dad. 'We've already moved her. We didn't want to distress Marble by leaving her there.'

'I'll go and see Marble then.'

'I'll finish off the cubicle shed,' said James, standing quickly. 'There's still quite a bit to do.'

Mandy opened the door of the calf box quietly. Marble was nuzzling at the surviving calf. The sight of it made Mandy's heart almost catch in her throat.

She reached out to stroke Marble's nose. She wondered if she knew that her calf was dead.

The surviving calf was still looking lively and bright-eyed. And Mandy knew, in exactly the same way that she'd known the other calf would die, that this one would live.

'You're a survivor, aren't you?' she said. 'And I think you're just about ready for your next feed by the look of you.'

Mandy smiled. When animals died it was always sad. But it was also a joy to see them grow stronger and live. It gave her hope.

'Just like my name,' she murmured to the calf. 'Mandy Hope. I guess it suits me.'

The calf blinked back at her.

Eight

Next morning Mandy woke early as she usually did. Her first thoughts were for Mr Matthews and Burnside Farm, especially for the little calf who hadn't pulled through. But she knew that it was the living calf which was important now; Mr Matthews would do everything he could to make sure that she survived.

Mandy jumped out of bed and pulled on her clothes. She had a busy day ahead. She thought about the jobs she had to do before she could go to Burnside Farm. There were her daily chores at Animal Ark, her rabbits to clean out and feed, and a visit with Dad to the riding-stables where he had several horses to look at.

When she got downstairs she found her mum and dad eating breakfast and discussing their plans for the day. Mandy shook cereal into a bowl and poured herself some orange juice.

'Don't forget to make yourself sandwiches if you're going up to Burnside Farm,' said Emily Hope. 'And could you take a couple of ready-made meals out of the freezer for Mr Matthews? If you put them in the cool-bag they should be all right until you get there.'

Mandy gulped down her juice and pushed back her chair.

'Thanks, Mum,' she said, stooping to give her mother a kiss on the cheek. 'Mr Matthews will appreciate it.'

'Why don't you sit down for five minutes,' said her dad, 'instead of dashing off like that?'

'I'd better get moving. There's a lot to do,' said Mandy, blowing him a kiss.

Adam Hope blew one back as Mandy ran out of the kitchen, banging the door behind her.

Jean Knox was already at reception when Mandy dashed through like a whirlwind. 'Morning, Mandy,' she called. 'I think Simon wants you to give him a hand. He's in the unit.'

Mandy pushed open the door to the residential unit. Simon was looking thoughtful, standing in front of one of the cages with a pair of thick gloves on his hand.

'Hi, Mandy. Do you fancy risking life and limb to help me with this little fellow?'

Mandy looked into the cage and saw a Pekinese dog staring out at her. 'He looks just like Pandora,' she said. 'It's not, is it, Simon?'

'Certainly not! Can you imagine Mrs Ponsonby leaving her darling Pandora all by herself? If Pandora had to stay in the residential unit Mrs Ponsonby would bring a sleeping-bag and lie down beside her.'

Mandy laughed. 'What's the problem?' she asked.

'I've got to take his stitches out and he tries to savage me every time I get near him. I think I'm going to ask your mum and dad for danger money!'

'He's not that bad, surely?'

But when she looked at Simon's serious face, she could see that he was.

'OK, so you need my help,' Mandy said. 'What do you want me to do?'

'When I lift him on to the treatment table can

you manage to tie his jaws together with that gauze? Make a big loop with it and then try to slot it over his head.'

'Will do,' said Mandy, picking up the roll of white gauze from the table.

As soon as Simon opened the door of the cage, the little dog sprang forward, snapping and snarling. When Simon picked him up, quickly and expertly, the dog continued to wriggle and squirm like a mad thing. For a minute or so, Mandy thought Simon was going to drop him. But he was too skilful for that. With his heavily gloved hands, Simon transferred the animal to the table and held him firmly so that he could hardly move.

'Don't go too near,' Simon warned. 'Stand a good way back and try to loop the gauze round his jaws.'

Mandy did as she was told. The first time she missed completely and the Pekinese went wild, trying to snap at the gauze. The next time she managed to get the loop round the dog's jaws.

'Pull tight!' Simon ordered.

Mandy pulled and tightened the gauze, tying it twice in two firm knots. The dog struggled again but there was nothing he could do. Mandy and Simon were safe!

'Here, you put these on, then you can hold him while I take the stitches out.'

Mandy took the gloves from Simon. They were enormous!

'I don't think for a minute you'll need them,' said Simon. 'That knot's pretty firm.'

'What happened to him?' asked Mandy.

'He managed to roll on some broken glass in a field.'

'Why are people so careless?' asked Mandy. 'It's so easy to injure an animal like that.'

Simon nodded in agreement.

Mandy held the dog while Simon deftly removed several stitches from the dog's side. The dog squirmed and growled deep in his throat, but there was nothing he could do.

'There,' said Simon, giving the little dog a pat. 'All done and dusted, old chap.'

'I may as well clean his cage out now that he's tied up,' said Mandy. 'I'll put him on a lead and he can sit on the floor for a while.'

'He may as well stay there; his owner's picking him up this morning.'

It didn't take Mandy long to clear out the old bedding, wipe round the cage with disinfectant and put in fresh straw.

Simon quickly untied the gauze from the dog's jaws, and stepped smartly out of the way before it had time to realise what was happening. 'Free at last!' he said to the little dog. The dog glared at him.

'I don't think he likes you, Simon,' said Mandy, laughing.

Simon winked. 'Never mind, it's all in a day's work,' he said, as Mandy went off to see to her rabbits.

Mandy was through her chores in record time. Even so, she made time to have a quick word and a cuddle with each of the animals. There wasn't much point in cleaning out the cages if you didn't get a cuddle from the occupants. With the exception of the occasional bad-tempered Pekinese of course!

'Mandy, you ready?'

It was Mr Hope, back from a farm visit.

'OK, Dad. Right with you.'

Mandy put her bike in the back of the Land-rover. Mr Hope would give her a lift up to Burnside Farm when they'd finished at the stables, as he wanted to have a look at Marble and her calf. Mandy would need her bike to get back home again.

The drive up to the riding-stables went past Highfield Farm – the farm that was for sale. As Mr Hope's Land-rover drew level with the farm gate, Mandy noticed two figures standing close together, deep in conversation. It was Sam Western and another man whom Mandy didn't recognise.

'Giles Pardoe,' said her dad, as if reading Mandy's thoughts. 'He owns Highfield Farm.'

'Not for much longer,' said Mandy gloomily. 'I bet Mr Western manages to buy it, no matter how many other people might want to buy the farm.'

'Let's hope not,' said Dad.

'I hope Alan Matthews gets back in time for the auction,' said Mandy.

They were silent until they reached the short driveway to the riding-stables. Mandy jumped out of the Land-rover and went to open the gate so that Adam Hope could drive through. She closed it after him and then walked the rest of the way up to the stables.

It was just a routine visit and wouldn't take too long. Mr Hope was there to give influenza and tetanus injections to the horses.

Mandy always loved the stables. About a dozen horses were looking out over the tops of their stable doors. They reminded Mandy of old men sunning themselves in their doorways; a little community of horses.

'Where's Whisper?' Mandy asked Mrs Forsyth, the stable owner. Whisper was a beautiful dapple-grey mare who was as sweet and gentle as her name.

'Over there, look. End box.'

'Oh yes!' Mandy had missed her because the big black stallion next door had been leaning forward and blocking her view.

'Hello, Whisper. Hello, old girl.' Mandy went over with the pieces of apple she'd brought with her. She opened her hand out flat and let the horse take them. Her muzzle felt soft and tickled.

Mr Hope was quick with the injections. A rub of antiseptic on the horse's neck, a quick lunge with the needle, then another rub and the whole procedure was over within seconds. The horses hardly seemed to feel a thing. And after each horse had had its shots Mandy rewarded it from her little store of apple slices.

'I hope I'll be as good at injections as you are,' said Mandy. 'I don't think you hurt the horses at all.'

Mr Hope smiled. 'I'm sure that you'll be excellent,' he said. 'People will come from miles around, just to watch you!'

Mandy laughed. 'I don't think I'll be *that* good,' she said.

They waved goodbye to Mrs Forsyth and headed off for Burnside Farm. James was already there, in the calf box with Mr Matthews.

'Come and have a look at this,' James called, beckoning them over. He was grinning from ear to ear. There was obviously some good news to report!

'I'll be there in a minute!' she called. 'Mum's given me some things to put in the freezer for Mr Matthews.'

When she went into the calf box the little calf was standing unsteadily on its feet. Marble had her head down towards her, sniffing and encouraging. The calf's legs seemed to fold up and she landed in the straw again.

Mr Matthews stood her up once more. No one said a word; they were all too intent on watching the calf.

Mr Matthews squirted some milk from one of the cow's teats on to his hand. He smeared the milk over the calf's nose and mouth.

'That's so as she gets the taste and smell of her mother's milk,' he told Mandy and James. 'It'll encourage her to walk towards the mother and feed.'

Sure enough the little calf began to stagger and sway towards Marble's udder. Marble nosed her gently and Mr Matthews steadied her with his hands.

The calf staggered nearer and nearer. At last she came within sight and smell of the udder and she began to root for the teat. With Mr Matthews' help, she finally found it. Within seconds the calf was sucking away as if it was something she'd been doing for years. Mandy felt like cheering.

'It's important that the calf gets her mother's milk as soon as possible,' Mr Matthews explained. 'It has antibodies in it which help to protect the calf from disease.'

'Well, she's doing great, John,' said Mr Hope. 'I think you may well be out of the woods with this one.'

Mandy smiled. It was the best news she'd heard for a long time!

'We only need your arm to get better, then everything will be just fine,' said Mandy.

'Oh, it's mending nicely. I'll be fit as a fiddle in a day or two.'

Mr Hope quickly checked Marble's surgery. 'It's

healing nicely,' he said. 'And Marble's looking good and healthy.'

Mandy felt so relieved. It looked as though mother, baby and farmer were going to be absolutely fine!

Mr Hope had to leave straight away; he'd promised to visit an injured badger at Betty Hilder's animal sanctuary. As Mandy waved him off she noticed another car coming down the drive. Gran and Grandad!

'We thought we might find you here,' said Grandad, as he climbed out of the car.

'And we were right,' added Gran, struggling to pull two baskets from the back seat. 'More supplies,' she said, handing Mandy one of the baskets.

'He's certainly not going to starve,' said Mandy, with a pleased smile. It was good to know that Mr Matthews was being looked after properly. At this rate he'd be able to have a banquet!

'Who's that?' asked Grandad, looking up the farm drive and shading his eyes with his hand.

'Looks like Lydia Fawcett,' said Gran.

'It is,' said Mandy, spotting Lydia's sturdy figure walking down the drive.

Mr Matthews and James emerged from the calf

box just as Lydia reached the farmyard.

'Well, my goodness,' said Mr Matthews. 'It looks like visiting time! I think I'd better put the kettle on.'

'Not a chance,' Gran said firmly. 'You go and put your feet up for an hour and entertain your guests. I'll get on with lunch.'

'You Hopes are certainly bossy,' said Mr Matthews, with a wink at Mandy. 'I can see where young Mandy gets it from.'

Everyone laughed. Lydia held out yet another basket, pulling aside a tea-towel to reveal more food. 'Some of my goats' cheese and a loaf I baked this morning. I thought you could do with it.'

'Bless you, Lydia. Bless all of you. You're very kind.'

Mr Matthews' eyes looked a bit moist, Mandy thought. She wondered if he was going to burst into tears!

But he didn't. 'Forward march!' he said decisively. 'Into the kitchen for the feast.'

They were all halfway through a delicious meal when Mandy heard yet another car draw up. A car door slammed, followed by a knock on the cottage door.

'More visitors,' said Mr Matthews, rising from

the table. 'I've never been so popular!'

It was Steve Barker, one of Sam Western's farm hands! He looked a bit sheepish when Mr Matthews invited him into the kitchen for a cup of tea.

'It's my day off,' he began, 'so I thought I'd see if you needed a hand. I know things have been a struggle just lately.'

Grandad pulled up another chair. Steve sat down and took the cup of tea which Gran had poured for him.

'I'd appreciate it if you didn't let Mr Western know that I've been here though.' He looked anxiously round the table. 'I don't think he'd be too pleased.'

'You're probably right,' said Grandad, grimly.

'We won't say a word,' said James.

'We certainly won't,' said Mandy.

'I felt ashamed when we met you on the road the other day,' Steve told Mandy. 'Ashamed of Mr Western, that is. And I want you to know that I don't agree with him. I think we should be helping our neighbours, not fighting them.'

'Aye, and pigs might fly as far as Sam Western is concerned,' said Mr Matthews.

Mandy had a sudden vision of Brandon Gill's

herd of pigs growing wings and taking to the air. That would be a sight to see!

Gran began to clear up the kitchen and Mr Matthews took everyone else outside and began directing operations like a military general. He had no problem in finding a job for everyone. It was a great help having Steve Barker there because he was a dairy man and knew the job inside out.

Mr Matthews breathed a big sigh of relief. 'At last I'll be able to catch up on some of those jobs that have been neglected for such a long time.'

Mandy and James were wandering over to the cubicle shed to clean the cubicles out once more.

'I'll have muscles like Mr Universe at this rate,' said James, picking up the big sweeping brush.

Mandy laughed. She tried to imagine skinny James with muscles, and failed. But after about half an hour of sweeping the cubicles she thought that she might develop bulging muscles too!

'Hey, look who's here!' called James.

Mandy turned to see Mr Matthews opening the gate to the cubicle shed. Walter Pickard and Ernie Bell were following him.

'More helpers!' shouted Mr Matthews.

Suddenly the whole thing seemed hilariously funny to Mandy. She couldn't help laughing as she thought of herself and James, Gran and Grandad, Lydia Fawcett, Steve Barker, and now Walter Pickard and Ernie Bell. It seemed as though the whole of Welford had come to Burnside Farm that day!

'You'll have to have a competition for the best helper,' Mandy said to Mr Matthews.

'Well, we all know who'd win, don't we?' said Mr Matthews, winking at Mandy and James.

'I've got the very special job of shifting the manure,' said Walter Pickard to Mandy and James. 'I used to help out on a farm before I went to be a butcher, but it's years since I last drove a tractor.'

'I hope you haven't forgotten how!' said James.

'It's like riding a bicycle,' said Mr Pickard. 'Once learned, never forgotten. At least I hope that's the case.'

'And I shall be doing my usual carpentering,' said Ernie Bell, glumly. He always looked that way, no matter what was happening. Mandy wondered what it would take to put a smile on his face, although she knew he had a heart of gold under his glum expression.

'Yes, some of the sheds and boxes need repairs, and there's some fencing needs looking at. You're going to be a great help, Ernie,' said Mr Matthews.

But Ernie Bell still looked glum!

Mandy and James had just returned to their jobs, and Walter Pickard had started up the tractor, when they heard the most enormous commotion of barking dogs. Mandy's heart sank. She didn't need to be told what was happening!

Everyone came rushing into the farmyard at the same time: Gran and Grandad, Mr Matthews, Mandy and James, Walter, Ernie, Lydia and Steve. It was like Picadilly Circus!

There was Sam Western, his dogs dancing round his heels, snapping and snarling at anyone who came near. Not that anyone dared get too near to the fierce animals. Even Mandy felt nervous of them.

'I've told you before,' said Mr Matthews quietly. 'Get those animals on a lead or I shall have to call the police.'

'Threats now, is it?' said Sam Western, smoothly. He turned to Steve Barker and his voice changed. It was low and nasty. 'You're fired, Steve Barker,' he said. 'I never want to see you on my farm again!'

Nine

Everyone looked stunned. Especially Steve Barker. Mr Matthews went and put his arm round his shoulders. 'Don't worry, lad. He'd be a fool to lose you.'

Steve didn't say anything, just shrugged his shoulders and looked at the ground.

Mandy was so enraged about Sam Western that she hardly knew what to do with herself. She swept the rest of the cubicles so vigorously that there wasn't a stray bit of sawdust left!

Later, everyone sat round the kitchen table looking extremely glum. Mandy thought how different it was from lunch-time, when they all had been so happy.

'I wish I could offer you something at High Cross Farm,' said Lydia. 'But there's only just enough work for me.'

'Don't worry,' said Steve. 'Something will turn up.' But he didn't look at all certain.

'Well, I'd better get these cups washed up,' said Gran. 'We'll need to be getting back soon.'

Just then the telephone rang. Mr Matthews ambled over to the dresser and lifted the receiver. 'Alan! Is that you? Good to hear from you, son. What's that you say? Are you sure? Absolutely sure? Well, that's marvellous! Marvellous! Yes, I'm fine, I'm fine. Don't worry about me.'

Mandy watched Mr Matthews during the telephone call. It was as though all the lines in his face had been suddenly smoothed out. His face was radiant with happiness.

'Good news?' she asked, when he finally put the phone down.

Mr Matthews came over to her chair, bent down, and kissed her. Mandy felt herself blush. But everyone was too busy looking at Mr Matthews to notice.

'I'll say it's good news! Alan's finally got everything sorted out in Australia. The money from my aunt's will has been released and there's enough to cover the purchase of Highfield Farm!'

There was a great chorus of cheers, and suddenly everyone was clapping as though Mr Matthews had just given an important speech. His face glowed red with pleasure. 'Goodness knows what time it was in Australia; I think Alan's been working nights to get this business sorted out.'

'Well, it was obviously worth the effort,' said Gran.

Mr Matthews smiled. 'I must get on,' he said. 'It's nearly milking time.'

'But Ted Wilkins is coming,' said James.

'Aye, but I still need to be there.'

Everyone started to leave the kitchen to get on with their jobs. Gran and Grandad had to go, and so did Lydia, who had her own animals to attend to. Mandy and James waved them all off from the yard.

'Milking time,' said Mr Matthews. 'I think you two wanted to help, if I'm not mistaken?'

'Yes, please!' said Mandy.

But she and James rushed off to have a look at the new calf first. 'We haven't seen her for at least two hours,' said Mandy.

When they leaned over the door of the calf box,

they found her much steadier on her feet and feeding contentedly. 'Isn't she grand?' said Mr Matthews, walking up behind them. 'She's got a new name now, you know.'

'Has she?' said Mandy.

'What is it?' asked James.

'She's called Mandy,' said Mr Matthews, with a smile. 'Are you two coming? The cows won't wait all day to be milked, you know.'

Mandy felt her heart swell with pleasure. *Mandy*! She felt so proud that she'd had a calf named after her.

'If the other one had lived, and it had been a boy, I'm sure Mr Matthews would have called him James,' she said.

'It's all right,' said James. 'I'm not jealous.' He gave Mandy a playful punch on the arm and they ran across the yard to the milking shed.

Ted Wilkins was already there, cleaning the cows' udders with a cloth and a bucket of water.

'It's important that the udders are clean, so we use a mixture of hypochlorite and detergent to make sure,' he told Mandy and James. 'Milk is a food, so we have to be very careful that everything's as clean and germ-free as possible.'

The cows knew exactly what they were doing.

Mandy and James watched, fascinated, as they queued up, waiting their turn to be milked. There was a sort of one-way traffic system. As soon as a cow had finished being milked, she stepped off the platform into a corridor that led from the back of the milking stalls into the cubicle shed. When the cow at the head of the queue saw that a stall was empty, she ambled along to it and climbed up. Sometimes Mr Matthews had to encourage a dreamy one, but usually they moved forward by themselves.

'It's amazing,' said James. 'They know exactly what to do!'

'They've had a good deal of practice,' said Ted, with a laugh. He was squirting milk from a cow's udder on to his hand.

'Why are you doing that?' Mandy wanted to know.

'It's to make sure there are no small clots of milk. If there are it's a sign of infection and the milk has to be thrown away.'

'What a shame,' said James.

'As I said: milk's a food and we can't afford to take any risks with hygiene. Of course it breaks a farmer's heart to throw it away. It's both food and money down the drain. Now then, you two. Could you fill up the food containers for me?'

Mandy and James picked up a bucket of cattle cake each and went round to the back of the milking stalls to fill up the food containers. The cows fed from these as they were being milked, chewing contentedly to the gentle rhythm of the milking machines.

'The machines sound as if they're saying "See-pop, see-pop, see-pop, see-pop",' said Mandy.

James listened carefully. 'Yes, they do,' he said. 'That's just what it sounds like.'

'Now, would you like to really help?' asked Mr Matthews. 'Ted, you show James what to do, and I'll help young Mandy.'

Mandy felt a thrill of excitement as one of the cows came to take her place on the milking platform. 'Now then,' said Mr Matthews, 'First thing you have to do is clean the teats. Let's see you do it.'

Mandy dipped the cloth into the bucket of cleaning solution and wrung it out. Carefully, and a little bit nervously, she took hold of one of the cow's teats and wiped it with the cloth. It felt strange at first, but she soon got the hang of it.

'Now then, squirt some milk into your hand and check it for clots.'

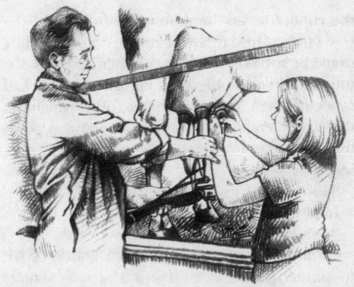

Mr Matthews showed her the proper way to pull at a cow's teat to get the milk. At first nothing came, but after one or two tries, she felt a trickle of warm milk running into her hand. She examined it carefully.

'It's fine, isn't it?'

Mr Matthews nodded. 'Now you can attach the jetters to the teats.'

'Jetters?'

Mr Matthews showed her. The jetters were part of the milking equipment and looked like four black rubber rings. They were attached by metal tubes to an enormous glass jar. Mandy saw how the rubber jetters were attached to each of the cow's teats. Mr Matthews explained how the milk would be sucked into these and then up the metal tube and into the big glass jar. The jar also had tubes attached. These led up into pipes which ran the whole length of the milking shed and down into the enormous metal container where the milk was collected.

'How do you know when the udder's empty?' asked Mandy.

'Wait and see,' said Mr Matthews.

Mandy watched. After a while, the jetters began to detach themselves from the cow's teats automatically!

'Clever, isn't it?' said Mr Matthews.

'It's amazing,' said Mandy.

'The jetters can detect when the flow of milk is getting less, and then they just detach themselves.'

Mr Matthews showed Mandy how to disinfect the teats after milking. 'The holes in the teats don't close up until about ten minutes after milking,' he told her. 'And that's when infection can get in. So it's important that the teats are disinfected, to stop that happening.'

'That's a huge amount of milk she's given,' said Mandy, eying the milk in the glass jar.

'Aye. A good milker can give up to sixteen thousand pints a year.'

Sixteen thousand pints! Mandy tried to imagine what sixteen thousand bottles of milk would look like. They'd probably stretch all the way from Animal Ark up to Burnside Farm!

As the next cow was climbing up on to the milking platform, Mandy saw Ted Wilkins pouring a whole bucket of milk down the drain. 'What are you doing that for?' she gasped.

'See that?' Ted pointed to a red mark that had been painted on one of the cow's flanks. Mandy nodded. 'That means she's on antibiotics to treat an infection. Humans musn't drink milk from cows that are receiving treatment so we have to throw the milk away.'

After all the cows had been milked, the milking apparatus and the milking shed itself had to be cleaned. Hypochlorite solution was sucked through all the pipes and equipment to clean it, then the floor and stalls of the milking shed were swilled with the same solution and brushed with a stiff yard brush. This was Mandy and James's job. The floor sloped slightly so that all the water could run down a little channel and into the drain.

'Well done, you two,' said Mr Matthews.

'We really enjoyed it,' said James.

'Good,' said Mr Matthews, rubbing at his arm.

'How is it?' asked Mandy.

'It's a lot better; thank you, Mandy. It's starting to itch now so that's a sign that it's healing. Dr Mason seems to be pleased with it anyway.'

'Shall we make you a drink when we've finished in here?' James asked.

'Not just now; thank you, James. Walter Pickard and Steve Barker have gone down to the bottom field to help Ernie with some fencing. I'm just going to join them.'

'See you tomorrow then,' said Mandy. 'We'll go when we've finished in here.'

Mr Matthews waved goodbye and was gone. Mandy and James carried on with the sweeping and swilling.

'I think we should take some tea over to them,' said James, when they'd finished in the milking shed.

'Good idea,' said Mandy. 'I saw a Thermos flask in the kitchen.'

Mandy made the tea while James fed the animals. Westie and the two cats were dancing round their feet and gave them no option. 'It's either feed them or trip over them,' said Mandy.

They decided to walk to the bottom field rather than taking their bikes. When they got there, all four men were busy working on different sections of fencing.

'Angels of mercy,' said Walter Pickard, spotting the flask and mugs.

Mandy and James decided to join them, and the six friends sat on the grass drinking tea.

'This is the life,' Walter Pickard said with a sigh.

Steve Barker said nothing. He sat, frowning and serious, slowly sipping at his tea.

'We ought to go,' said James, collecting the mugs. 'I've got to walk Blackie and there's a holiday project for school which I haven't even started yet.'

Mandy and James said goodbye and strolled back towards the farmyard. They were about two hundred metres from the back of the farmhouse when Mandy spotted a little white blur racing towards them.

'Westie!'

Mandy bent down to stroke him but he was far too excited to stay still. He barked and ran round in circles, his ears erect and sharp.

'What's the matter, Westie?' Mandy asked.

'How did he get out?' asked James.

'Come on,' said Mandy. 'I think we'd better go

and investigate. I've got a feeling that something's wrong.'

The two of them ran the short distance back to the farmyard. Westie ran ahead of them, stopping every now and then to check that Mandy and James were following. When they drew into the farmyard it was much, much worse than they'd feared. Not only was the cottage door wide open, but so was the door to every shed and calving box! Marble was standing in the yard looking completely lost.

'I'll get her back in the box,' said Mandy.

'And I'll put Westie in the kitchen,' said James.

Westie didn't like being shut in the kitchen. He barked and barked. 'Sorry old boy, no time to stop,' said James.

'James, the calf's gone! She's not in here!'

James ran across the yard to look. Mandy was right; there was only Marble in the stall.

'What's going on, James? Who could have left all the doors open?'

'I don't know.' James shook his head. He was as puzzled as Mandy.

The two friends checked all the calf boxes. Some of the calves had wandered out but others had stayed put. They closed and bolted the doors and tried to round up the stray calves. It took them ages; some of the calves were enjoying their freedom! But at last they had all the calves back in the boxes. All except for Marble's calf.

'Oh, James. What's happened to her?' Mandy was close to tears. 'Where on earth can she be?'

'I wonder if she could have got into the cubicle shed?' he answered.

'But how? She can hardly walk yet,' said Mandy.

Even so, the two of them dashed off to the cubicle shed to have a look. Mandy's heart was pounding and her mouth was dry with fear.

James, two strides ahead of her, pushed open the gate to the cubicle shed. There wasn't a cow in sight!

Ten

'You run back and get the others,' Mandy gasped. 'I'll start looking.'

James didn't stop to argue. By the time Mandy had decided where to start looking, he had gone.

Mandy remembered there was an old brick outhouse with a flight of steps running up the outside of the building. From there she ought to get a pretty good view of the fields behind the cottage.

It was only a matter of seconds before she found herself at the top of the steps. She ran her eyes over the fields, but all she could see was the little group of people helping Ernie Bell with the fencing.

She ran down and back across the yard towards the long farm drive. What she saw there made her heart turn over. A long trail of cows was ambling slowly up the drive towards the main road. If somebody didn't stop them now, one of them might get killed!

Mandy didn't have time to think. She ran like lightning down the drive towards the line of cattle. As the cows at the back of the group heard her footsteps they glanced around uneasily. The others sensed danger and began to scatter. Two or three cows at the head of the trail even began to run!

Don't panic, thought Mandy. She climbed over the fence that bordered the driveway and ran along the grass. It was slower but much quieter.

She found herself drawing level with the cow at the front of the herd. She almost leaped over the fence and back on to the drive. She stood facing the cows. They had started to slow down almost as soon as Mandy had gone on to the grass, no longer frightened by her pounding footsteps on the tarmac behind them.

Mandy stood with her arms and legs out-stretched, trying to make herself as wide as possible in order to block the cows' way. Gradually she started to move forward, making sure that her movements were smooth in order not to frighten the cows further.

To her relief the cows began to move backwards as she moved towards them; back towards the safety of the farmyard.

They were progressing steadily nearer when Mandy saw reinforcements ahead. James, together with Mr Matthews and Walter Pickard, was walking quietly up the drive at the side of the cows, being careful not to startle them.

As they came nearer, Mandy could hear Mr Matthews talking gently to the cows. His voice was soothing and they seemed to respond to him.

At last James and the men reached the head of the herd.

'Well done, Mandy,' said Mr Matthews. Quietly and firmly he began to encourage the cows back down the drive. Steve Barker and Ernie Bell had stayed at the other end of the drive to herd the cows back across the yard and into the cubicle shed.

Within minutes all the cows were accounted for. Mr Matthews went round all of them, counting and checking that none was missing. The only one they couldn't find was Marble's calf.

Mr Matthews shook his head. Mandy could see

the worry and strain on his face.

'I think you should phone the police,' said Steve Barker. 'Someone has deliberately let your cattle loose, and it looks as though they may have stolen a calf.'

And I bet I know just who it was, thought Mandy. That Sam Western was a nasty piece of work! She looked at James and she could see that he was thinking exactly the same. Not that she'd known Sam Western to steal before. But perhaps if he was desperate enough to get Highfield Farm, he might do just that!

'Come on, let's go inside and have a drink,' said Walter Pickard. 'I think we all need one.'

Westie had begun barking again as soon as he heard everyone come into the yard. And he was still barking now.

They trooped towards the kitchen door, Mandy and James in the lead. Mandy was close to tears. To think of all the love and attention that had been lavished on the little calf, and now someone had stolen her!

But when Mandy walked into the cottage she had the shock of her life. No wonder Westie was barking so frantically. Lying on the rug in front of the fire was the calf! She lifted her head at the sound of the door opening, and tried to scramble to her feet as Mandy and James came towards her.

'Mandy!' shouted Mandy Hope. 'How did you get in here?' She and James were down on their knees petting and stroking the little animal. Mandy put her arms round the calf's neck and gave her a big hug. 'You beautiful, naughty little calf!'

'I think someone must have brought her in,' said James. 'She'd never have managed by herself.'

'Yes, and I've a good idea who that person might be,' said Steve Barker.

'Mr Western?' asked Mandy. Steve nodded.

The calf finally stood up, looked around her, and trotted over to the open window. She poked her head out just as Mr Matthews was walking past!

'Well!' said Mr Matthews, in astonishment. 'I know I love my animals but I've never had a calf in the cottage before!'

Everyone laughed. But then it was action stations again!

Walter Pickard busied himself making a large jug of squash, while Steve Barker volunteered to phone the police.

'Don't bother, Steve. There was no damage

done,' said Mr Matthews, back in the kitchen once more.

He knelt down and lifted the calf on to his shoulders. She was draped around his neck like a scarf! Mr Matthews carefully held on to her legs so that she wouldn't fall. 'I think this young lady needs to go and see her mother,' he said.

'She's not the only one!' said James.

'I'll give you a lift home if you like,' Ernie Bell offered. There was enough room in the back of Ernie's van to hold the two bikes, so Mandy and James were able to accept.

They hardly spoke on the way home; they were too busy yawning. It had been an exhausting day!

James had suggested that they meet outside McFarlane's post office the following day. He still hadn't started his project and he wanted to get on with it. Mandy had homework to do too, so it seemed a good idea to do it then.

She found it difficult to make a start. She'd much rather be helping to look after the animals at Burnside Farm. But she knew that if she didn't work hard at school then she wouldn't be able to be a vet, and she wanted that more than anything in the world.

By lunch-time, she'd finished all of her English and history and had made a start on the science project. She was more than satisfied.

Mum had made vegetable soup for lunch, and they ate this with salad and cheese. It was delicious!

'Did I tell you that Mr Matthews has named the new calf after me?'

'Only about three times,' said Adam Hope.

'Dad!'

Mr Hope grinned at her from behind his newspaper. 'Talking of Mr Matthews, there's an announcement in the paper about the auction of Highfield Farm. It's on Friday.'

'Friday!' said Mandy. Her heart sank. Would Alan Matthews get back from Australia in time? It was already Wednesday; there were only two days left!

'What do you think will happen if Mr Western gets Highfield Farm?' she asked her parents.

'Well, if he does, let's just hope he leaves Mr Matthews in peace,' said Mrs Hope.

Mandy frowned. She couldn't imagine that happening.

'And don't forget that Alan and Mr Matthews will have a lot of money soon. They'll be able to improve Burnside Farm even if they don't buy Highfield.'

Mandy sighed. Perhaps her mum was right. There was no point in worrying about something that hadn't even happened yet. She pushed her chair back from the table and began to clear away the dishes. She was going to be late meeting James if she didn't get a move on.

'Hey, what's the rush?' said Simon, as Mandy almost knocked him over in the reception area.

'Sorry!' Mandy shouted from the front door. 'Got to dash!'

James was already waiting when she got to the post office.

They were just about to cycle off when Mandy pulled back. 'Hang on a minute, James.'

Walking towards them was the woman with the beautiful Great Dane who Mandy had met coming out of the surgery.

'Hello,' said Mandy. 'I'm Mandy Hope. The vets' daughter from Animal Ark.'

The woman's puzzled expression cleared. 'Oh, yes; I remember.'

'How's your dog?' asked Mandy, leaning forward to stroke him. He was a beautiful animal.

'Oh, he's doing very well; aren't you, Tiny?'

'Tiny!' Mandy nearly fell off her bike with laughing. The woman laughed too, and then proceeded to tell Mandy all about the difficult decision she'd had to make about whether to take her dog abroad.

'So we've decided to take him with us,' the woman said. 'It's such a relief. I just couldn't bear to lose him. Not after ten years. He's one of the family.'

Tiny gave an enormous yawn, as if he found the whole subject exceedingly boring!

''Bye then,' said Mandy. 'Good luck!'

Mandy and James set off at last. But they were just cycling past the Fox and Goose when they saw Walter Pickard. He waved at them to slow down.

'Have you young ones heard the good news?' he asked. It was obvious that they hadn't, so Mr Pickard told them. 'Alan Matthews is coming home. He'll be back tomorrow in time for the auction!'

'Yes!' Mandy and James cheered.

'This is a day for good news,' said Mandy, as they waved goodbye to Walter Pickard. 'First the Great Dane, and now this. I've got a feeling everything's going to turn out well.'

When they got to Burnside Farm, Mr Matthews was beaming from ear to ear. 'Have you heard?

Have you heard?' He was almost dancing! 'I've arranged a celebration lunch for Friday, just before the auction. At the Fox and Goose. Will you come?'

Would they come? Of course they would!

'It's by way of a thank-you to all the good friends who've helped me out. And you two are top of the list!'

'Pity we can't take the other Mandy too,' said James, grinning.

'Oh yes, I can just imagine a little brown and white calf sitting up at the table with a bib round her neck,' said Mandy.

'We could sit Blackie next to her,' said James. 'And Eric.'

They were all laughing as they made their way across the yard to the calf box.

Mandy the calf was feeding from her mother, her tail wagging. 'I think that's the sort of meal she likes best,' said James.

'That's a sign of a healthy calf,' said Mr Matthews.

'Come on, tail-wagger,' said Mandy, holding out her hand as the calf stopped feeding.

'She's inquisitive, you see,' said Mr Matthews. 'They're like human babies; they're curious about everything.'

James took a step towards her and the calf skittered round the box on her long spindly legs.

'She's getting much steadier on her legs,' said James.

'Stay still and she'll come,' Mr Matthews advised.

And she did. She started to suck at Mandy's hand and Mandy laughed with delight. 'As long as she doesn't try to chew it!' she said.

The day of the auction dawned bright and sunny. When Mandy arrived at the Fox and Goose with her parents, she found James waiting outside for them.

'I didn't want to go in on my own,' he said, going a bit red.

'I don't blame you,' said Emily Hope. 'It looks as though there are an awful lot of people in there.'

There were! Mr Matthews had reserved a huge table right in the middle of the restaurant area. Around it sat Mr Matthews with his son, Alan, looking very brown after his trip to Australia, Lydia Fawcett, Ernie Bell, Walter Pickard, Steve Barker and Gran and Grandad!

'I make that twelve people all together,' said James.

'Aye, it's a grand party,' said Mr Matthews.

And it was. It was a real celebration. The food was delicious too!

'I don't think I'm ever going to eat again,' said Mandy at the end of the meal.

'I'll believe that when I see it!' said Mrs Hope, with a smile.

Both Adam and Emily Hope had visits to make and had to leave as soon as they'd eaten.

'Why not come to the auction?' said Mr Matthews, to Mandy and James. 'It'll be an experience.'

And it was! The sale room in Walton was a large place that had vast high windows and smelled of polish. There was a large crowd of people and Mandy and James recognised quite a lot of them. Including Sam Western, who sat near the front, looking as unconcerned as if he was just off to buy fish and chips, instead of an expensive farm.

Mr Matthews looked nervous, Mandy noticed. He was fidgeting in his chair and kept clearing his throat. Alan Matthews looked at his father and gave him a thumbs-up sign.

'Here's the auctioneer,' said James, pointing to a man at the front of the room. He climbed on to a sort of stage and stood high up holding a wooden hammer.

Soon the auction was in full swing. Mandy was astonished that nobody except the auctioneer actually spoke. People just raised their hands or made other signs that the auctioneer seemed to understand.

Mr Western seemed constantly on the move, raising his hand and nodding his head. He kept turning to look at Alan Matthews. If Mandy hadn't known what a cool customer Sam Western was, she would have thought that he was actually nervous.

Alan Matthews was busy too. His hand kept going up and his face was gleaming with sweat. He cast worried glances at Mr Western.

As the price for Highfield Farm rose higher, Mandy and James saw that everyone else had dropped out, and only Alan Matthews and Sam Western were still bidding. Mr Western's face was getting redder and redder.

Things were moving so fast now that it was difficult to know quite what was happening. At last, though, they heard the auctioneer bang his hammer and announce that Highfield Farm was sold!

'Who to?' asked Mandy, her heart racing.

'To me and young Alan,' said Mr Matthews.

'We're the proud new owners of Highfield Farm!'

Mr Matthews bent and kissed Mandy on the cheek, then leaned across to shake hands with James.

Everyone crowded round to congratulate Alan and Mr Matthews. Everyone except Sam Western.

On the way out of the auction room he gave Mr Matthews a cold, hard look. 'I think I've had a lucky escape,' he said. 'Farming next to you would not have been pleasant.'

Then he turned to Steve Barker. 'And as for you; you'll never work on a farm in this district again. Not if I have anything to do with it.'

'Well, that shouldn't be a problem, Mr Western. Steve's coming to work for me and Alan. Aren't you, Steve?' Mr Matthews gave Steve a pat on the back.

Sam Western's face turned red with anger. But he didn't say another word. He just turned and strode out of the door.

'Phew!' said James.

Mandy was thrilled for Steve Barker. He wouldn't be out of work after all! And Mr Matthews and Alan could go on caring for animals at Burnside Farm.

Mandy thought of the little calf and she smiled

with happiness. Everything had turned out just perfectly!

Dear Reader,

I'm so pleased with the letters I have been receiving about **Animal Ark**. It seems there are a great number of fans of the series, and I am very happy that so many people are enjoying the books.

I especially enjoy reading your suggestions for new titles – so keep them coming!

Much love

Lucy Daniels

KOALAS IN A CRISIS
Animal Ark in Australia, 16

Lucy Daniels

Mandy longs to meet her first koala and she's not disappointed when she visits the wildlife sanctuary.

But her joy turns to horror when she learns that the baby koalas and their babies are threatened.

Can Mandy save the koalas from starvation?

ANIMAL ARK AS SEEN ON TV – LUCY DANIELS

70908 1	KITTENS IN THE KITCHEN	£3.50	☐
70911 1	PONY IN THE PORCH	£3.50	☐
70912 X	PUPPIES IN THE PANTRY	£3.50	☐
70913 8	GOAT IN THE GARDEN	£3.50	☐
71349 6	HEDGEHOGS IN THE HALL	£3.50	☐
70909 X	BADGER IN THE BASEMENT	£3.50	☐
71345 3	PIGLET IN A PLAYPEN	£3.50	☐
70914 6	BUNNIES IN THE BATHROOM	£3.50	☐
71346 1	DONKEY ON THE DOORSTEP	£3.50	☐
70910 3	HAMSTER IN A HAMPER	£3.50	☐
71350 X	GOOSE ON THE LOOSE	£3.50	☐
71347 X	CALF IN THE COTTAGE	£3.50	☐
71348 8	GUINEA PIG IN THE GARBAGE	£3.50	☐

All Hodder Children's books are available at your local bookshop or newsagent, or can be ordered direct from the publisher. Just tick the titles you want and fill in the form below. Prices and availability subject to change without notice.

Hodder Children's Books, Cash Sales Department, Bookpoint, 39 Milton Park, Abingdon, OXON, OX14 4TD, UK. If you have a credit card you may order by telephone – (01235) 831700.

Please enclose a cheque or postal order made payable to Bookpoint Ltd to the value of the cover price and allow the following for postage and packing:

UK & BFPO – £1.00 for the first book, 50p for the second book, and 30p for each additional book ordered up to a maximum charge of £3.00.

OVERSEAS & EIRE – £2.00 for the first book, £1.00 for the second book, and 50p for each additional book.

Name ....

Address ....

....

....

If you would prefer to pay by credit card, please complete:
Please debit my Visa/Access/Diner's Card/American Express (delete as applicable) card no:

Signature ....

Expiry Date ....